PROTECTING HUMAN RIGHTS OF REFUGEES
Issues & International Intervention

PROTECTING HUMAN RIGHTS OF REFUGEES

Issues & International Intervention

Sarat C. Joshi

FORWARD BOOKS
NEW DELHI • GUWAHATI • VISAKHAPATNAM

FORWARD BOOKS
4649-B/21, Ansari Road
Darya Ganj, New Delhi - 110 002
Ph.: 23263193 / 9811582579 / 09435116718
Fax: 011-23263193
Email: ektabooks@yahoo.com
www.akanshapublishinghouse.com

Protecting Human Rights of Refugees: Issues & International Intervention

First Published 2011

ISBN 978-81-909742-5-7

[The responsibility for the facts stated, conclusions reached etc., is entirely that of the author. The publisher is not responsible for them, whatsoever.]

PRINTED IN INDIA

Published by Forward Books, New Delhi and Printed at S.N. Printers, Delhi.

Contents

CONTENTS

PREFACE

> "When a poor fool acquires riches he become a rich fool."
>
> —*Abraham Miller*

Refugee problem is a global problem, infesting all countries of the world. Basically, refugee is a person who, owing to persecution or well-founded fear of persecution for reasons of race, colour, religion, political belief or membership of a particular social group; (a) leaves the state of which he is a national or the country of his nationality, or, if he has no nationality, the state or the country of which he is a habitual resident, or (b) being outside such state or country, is unable or unwilling to return to it or avail himself of its protection.

The present work intends to address all crucial issues concerned with the refugee problem in entirety All these are given an elaborate treatment, besides this some important and elevant national/international instruments for protecting basic human rights of refugees are also given. The vital and useful information is gathered under the following chapters—Introduction; Refugee Concept in International Law; UNHCR: Responsibilities and Concern; Refugees in SAARC Region; Major Human Rights Instruments; Convention Relating to the Status of Refugees; Protocol Relating to Status of Refugees (1967); Constitution of International Refugee Organization; Convention on the Reduction of Statelessness; Case Studies; Temporary Protection, Repatriation Aid and Development;

International Efforts for Refugee/Returnee Aid and Development; Appendices and Bibliography etc.

Primarily meant for students, researchers and academics in the field of political science, sociology, human rights and economics, this will equally serve the purpose of all social scientists, social and human rights activists, NGOs, policy planners and international agencies concerned with the cause of refugees.

For furnishing authentic picture of the theme, the relevant information is gathered from various official reports of different agencies, and organizations, articles, papers and monographs, prepared by various experts in the field. We are deeply beholden to them all. We express our greatfulness to our colleagues, and seniors, friends who have rendered all assistance and guidance while working on this project. Finally, I am thankful to my publishers for their interest and materializing this within stipulated time in elegant manner.

I will appreciate if constructive comments could be forwarded by learned users to enhance the quality of information contained herein, which I shall corroborate in the subsequent edition of the book with due acknowledgement.

—SCJ

1

INTRODUCTION

> "No condition or set of circumstances is in itself a calamity to be feared. It is our reaction to it that makes it a "Waterloo" or a field of triumph."
>
> *Auction—Auctions*

Basically, Refugee is a person who, owing to persecution or well-founded fear of persecution for reasons of race, colour, religion, political belief or membership of a particular social group; (a) leaves the state of which he is a national or the country of his nationality, or, if he has no nationality, the state or the country of which he is a habitual resident, or (b) being outside such state or country, is unable or unwilling to return to it or avail himself of its protection.

Prior to this century there was little concern about the precise definition of a refugee, since most of those who chose not to move to the "New World" were readily received by rulers in Europe and elsewhere. The practice of sheltering those compelled to flight was not perceived as a burden, but rather as a necessary incident of power, and indeed as a source of communal enrichment: Central governments pursued their own interests by facilitating immigration and discouraging or even forbidding emigration. Whether to be taxed, to contribute to the growth of manufactures and

REFUGEE POPULATION IN THE WORLD

Rank	*Country / Territory*	*Total Population*	*Refugee Population*	*Natives per Refugee*
–	**World**	**6,865,100,000**	**13,599,900**	**505**
1	*Palestine*	3,761,646	1,828,100	2
2	Jordan	6,316,000	621,600	10
3	Syria	21,906,000	1,763,900	12
4	Lebanon	4,224,000	333,500	13
5	Chad	11,206,000	330,500	34
6	Iran	74,196,000	993,600	75
7	Kuwait	2,985,000	40,000	75
8	Cyprus	801,600	10,000	80
9	Botswana	1,950,000	23,100	84
10	Saudi Arabia	25,721,000	291,100	88
11	Republic of the Congo	3,683,000	40,000	92
12	Pakistan	170,387,500	1,775,600	96
13	Djibouti	864,000	8,800	98
14	Ecuador	14,036,775	135,000	104
15	Kenya	39,802,000	377,400	105
16	Mauritania	3,291,000	30,600	108
17	Gabon	1,475,000	13,100	113
18	Gambia	1,705,000	14,900	114
19	Venezuela	28,456,383	211,000	135
20	Tanzania	43,739,000	321,900	136
21	Zambia	12,935,000	88,900	146
22	Serbia	9,850,000	66,600	148
23	Malaysia	27,468,000	171,500	160
24	Yemen	23,580,000	145,700	162
25	Rwanda	9,998,000	59,000	169
26	Thailand	63,389,730	368,800	172
27	Sudan	42,272,000	233,900	181
28	Namibia	2,171,000	11,700	186
29	South Africa	49,320,000	256,200	193
30	Guinea-Bissau	1,611,000	8,300	194
31	Panama	3,454,000	17,200	201
32	Uganda	32,710,000	155,400	210
33	Cameroon	19,522,000	91,900	212
34	Nepal	29,331,000	121,300	242

35	Costa Rica	4,579,000	18,600	246
36	Burundi	8,303,000	26,300	316
37	Greece	11,257,285	34,300	328
38	Sierra Leone	5,696,000	17,200	331
39	Libya	6,420,000	18.900	340
40	Dem. Rep. of Congo	66,020,000	192,700	343
41	Senegal	12,534,000	35,900	349
42	Guinea	10,069,000	28,100	358
43	Algeria	34,895,000	96,500	362
44	Norway	4,834,000	13,300	363
45	Sweden	9,292,359	23,400	397
46	Israel	7,434,000	16,500	451
48	Central African Republic	4,422,000	9,100	486
49	Egypt	77,116,112	152,400	506
50	Bosnia and Herzegovina	3,767,000	7,400	509
51	Switzerland	7,739,100	13,700	565
52	Ethiopia	79,221,000	135,200	586
53	Somalia	9,133,000	15,300	597
54	Republic of Macedonia	2,048,620	3,200	640
55	Papua New Guinea	6,732,000	10,000	673
56	Austria	8,355,260	12,200	685
57	Armenia	3,230,100	4,500	718
58	Iraq	30,747,000	39,500	778
59	Côte d'Ivoire	21,075,000	26,300	801
60	Spain	45,929,476	5,600	820
61	Bangladesh	162,221,000	193,100	840
62	Togo	6,619,000	6,900	959
63	Niger	15,290,000	15,700	974
64	Eritrea	5,073,000	5,000	1015
65	Benin	8,935,000	8,400	1064
66	Liberia	3,476,608	18,800	1064
67	Angola	18,498,000	15,900	1163
68	Mali	13,010,000	11,100	1172
70	Finland	5,343,608	4,200	1272
71	Ghana	23,837,000	18,700	1275
72	Malawi	15,263,000	11,600	1316
73	Russia	141,803,000	107,000	1325
74	Netherlands	16,535,207	11,800	1401

75	Germany	82,046,000	54,200	1514
76	Belgium	10,754,528	7,100	1515
77	Croatia	4,435,056	2,600	1706
78	Mozambique	22,894,000	12,900	1775
79	United States	310,101,000	161,200	1924
80	Denmark	5,519,441	2,800	1971
81	Australia	22,268,000	9,900	2249
82	United Kingdom	61,634,599	26,600	2317
83	India	1,183,610,000	411,000	2880
84	France	65,073,482	22,300	2918
85	Azerbaijan	8,629,900	2,800	3082
86	Italy	60,088,880	19,000	3163
87	Zimbabwe	12,523,000	3,900	3211
88	Czech Republic	10,467,542	3,200	3271
89	Kazakhstan	15,776,492	4,500	3506
90	Turkey	71,517,100	18,200	3930
91	People's Republic of China	1,339,450,000	332,000	4034
92	Poland	38,100,700	5,700	6684
93	Brazil	193,539,000	21,400	9044
94	Vietnam	85,789,573	9,500	9030
95	Nigeria	154,729,000	9,200	16818
96	South Korea	48,333,000	2,500	19333
97	Mexico	107,550,697	3,600	29875
98	Japan	127,590,000	3,100	41158
99	Indonesia	229,965,000	unknown	unknown
100	Philippines	92,222,660	unknown	unknown
101	Myanmar (Burma)	50,020,000	unknown	unknown
102	Ukraine	46,029,281	unknown	unknown
103	Colombia	45,064,807	unknown	unknown
104	Argentina	40,134,425	unknown	unknown
105	Morocco	31,567,613	unknown	unknown
106	Peru	29,132,013	unknown	unknown
107	Afghanistan	28,150,000	unknown	unknown
108	Uzbekistan	27,488,000	unknown	unknown
109	North Korea	24,051,706	unknown	unknown
110	Taiwan	23,069,345	unknown	unknown
111	Romania	21,498,616	unknown	unknown
112	Sri Lanka	20,238,000	unknown	unknown

113	Madagascar	19,625,000	unknown	unknown
114	Chile	17,121,000	unknown	unknown
115	Burkina Faso	15,757,000	unknown	unknown
116	Cambodia	14,805,000	unknown	unknown
117	Guatemala	14,027,000	unknown	unknown
118	Cuba	11,204,000	unknown	unknown
119	Portugal	10,627,250	unknown	unknown
120	Tunisia	10,327,800	unknown	unknown
121	Dominican Republic	10,090,000	unknown	unknown
122	Haiti	10,033,000	unknown	unknown
123	Hungary	10,031,208	unknown	unknown
124	Bolivia	9,863,000	unknown	unknown
125	Belarus	9,671,900	unknown	unknown
126	Bulgaria	7,606,551	unknown	unknown
127	Honduras	7,466,000	unknown	unknown
128	*Hong Kong*	7,008,900	unknown	unknown
129	Tajikistan	6,952,000	unknown	unknown
130	Paraguay	6,349,000	unknown	unknown
131	Laos	6,320,000	unknown	unknown
132	El Salvador	6,163,000	unknown	unknown
133	Nicaragua	5,743,000	unknown	unknown
134	Kyrgyzstan	5,482,000	unknown	unknown
135	Slovakia	5,413,548	unknown	unknown
136	Turkmenistan	5,110,000	unknown	unknown
137	Singapore	4,839,400	unknown	unknown
138	United Arab Emirates	4,599,000	unknown	unknown
139	Ireland	4,422,100	unknown	unknown
140	Georgia	4,385,400	unknown	unknown
141	New Zealand	4,365,000	unknown	unknown
142	*Puerto Rico*	3,982,000	unknown	unknown
143	Moldova	3,567,500	unknown	unknown
144	Uruguay	3,361,000	unknown	unknown
145	Lithuania	3,349,872	unknown	unknown
146	Albania	3,170,000	unknown	unknown
147	Oman	2,845,000	unknown	unknown
148	Jamaica	2,719,000	unknown	unknown
149	Mongolia	2,671,000	unknown	unknown
150	Latvia	2,257,300	unknown	unknown

151	Lesotho	2,067,000	unknown	unknown
152	Slovenia	2,045,249	unknown	unknown
153	Qatar	1,409,000	unknown	unknown
154	Estonia	1,340,415	unknown	unknown
155	Trinidad and Tobago	1,339,000	unknown	unknown
156	Mauritius	1,288,000	unknown	unknown
157	Swaziland	1,185,000	unknown	unknown
158	East Timor	1,134,000	unknown	unknown
159	Fiji	849,000	unknown	unknown
160	Bahrain	791,000	unknown	unknown
161	Guyana	762,000	unknown	unknown
162	Bhutan	697,000	unknown	unknown
163	Comoros	676,000	unknown	unknown
164	Equatorial Guinea	676,000	unknown	unknown
165	Montenegro	624,000	unknown	unknown
166	*Macau*	546,200	unknown	unknown
167	Solomon Islands	523,000	unknown	unknown
168	Suriname	520,000	unknown	unknown
169	*Western Sahara*	513,000	unknown	unknown
170	Cape Verde	506,000	unknown	unknown
171	Luxembourg	493,500	unknown	unknown
172	Malta	413,627	unknown	unknown
173	Brunei	400,000	unknown	unknown
174	Bahamas	342,000	unknown	unknown
175	Belize	322,100	unknown	unknown
176	Iceland	319,246	unknown	unknown
177	Maldives	309,000	unknown	unknown
178	Barbados	256,000	unknown	unknown
179	Vanuatu	240,000	unknown	unknown
180	*Netherlands Antilles*	198,000	unknown	unknown
181	Samoa	179,000	unknown	unknown
182	*Guam*	178,000	unknown	unknown
183	Saint Lucia	172,000	unknown	unknown
184	São Tomé and Príncipe	163,000	unknown	unknown
185	Federated States of Micronesia	111,000	unknown	unknown
186	*U.S. Virgin Islands*	110,000	unknown	unknown
187	Saint Vincent and the Grenadines	109,000	unknown	unknown
188	*Aruba*	107,000	unknown	unknown

189	Grenada	104,000	unknown	unknown
190	Tonga	104,000	unknown	unknown
191	Kiribati	98,000	unknown	unknown
192	*Jersey*	89,300	unknown	unknown
193	Antigua and Barbuda	88,000	unknown	unknown
194	*Northern Mariana Islands*	87,000	unknown	unknown
195	Andorra	86,000	unknown	unknown
196	Seychelles	84,000	unknown	unknown
197	*Isle of Man*	80,000	unknown	unknown
198	Dominica	67,000	unknown	unknown
199	*American Samoa*	67,000	unknown	unknown
200	*Bermuda*	65,000	unknown	unknown
201	Marshall Islands	62,000	unknown	unknown
202	*Guernsey*	61,811	unknown	unknown
203	*Greenland*	57,000	unknown	unknown
204	*Cayman Islands*	56,000	unknown	unknown
205	Saint Kitts and Nevis	52,000	unknown	unknown
206	*Faroe Islands*	48,940	unknown	unknown
207	Liechtenstein	35,593	unknown	unknown
208	Monaco	33,000	unknown	unknown
209	*Turks and Caicos Islands*	33,000	unknown	unknown
210	*Gibraltar*	31,000	unknown	unknown
211	San Marino	30,800	unknown	unknown
212	*British Virgin Islands*	23,000	unknown	unknown
213	*Cook Islands*	20,000	unknown	unknown
214	Palau	20,000	unknown	unknown
215	*Anguilla*	15,000	unknown	unknown
216	Tuvalu	10,000	unknown	unknown
217	Nauru	10,000	unknown	unknown
218	*Saint Helena*	6,600	unknown	unknown
219	*Montserrat*	5,900	unknown	unknown
220	*Falkland Islands*	3,000	unknown	unknown
221	*Niue*	1,500	unknown	unknown
222	*Tokelau*	1,400	unknown	unknown
223	Vatican City	800	unknown	unknown
224	*Pitcairn Islands*	50	unknown	unknown

Source: http://en.wikipedia.org/wiki/List _of _countries_ by_ refugee_ Population.

commerce, to offer specialized knowledge, or to join the military, talented or affluent foreigners were frequently deemed useful to society and welcomed with open arms by European monarchs or municipalities.

This freedom of international movement accorded to persons broadly defined as refugees was adversely impacted by the adoption of instrumentalist immigration policies in Western states during the early twentieth century. Immigration came to be seen less as a means of allowing individuals to exercise their right to self-determination, and more as a vehicle to facilitate the election by states of new inhabitants who could contribute in some tangible way, such as skill or wealth, to the national well-being. International migration was no longer to be a function of the particularized needs or ambitions of the would-be immigrants, but was instead to be closely controlled to maximize advantage for sovereign nation states.

The desire of European states to establish normative standards and control mechanisms to stem the arrival of immigrants perceived as noncontributing clashed head-on with the enormity of a series of major population displacements within Europe during the early part of the twentieth century. The most prominent migrations were the flight of more than one million Russians between 1917 and 1922, and the exodus during the early 1920s of hundreds of thousands of Armenians from Turkey in order to avoid persecution and massacre by the government of that country. The social crisis brought on by the de facto immigration of so many refugees convinced governments that their laws would have to recognize the reality of forced international movements of people. Because political and other disruptions would inevitably induce involuntary migration, policies of selecting immigrants on the basis -of national advantage alone were obliged to yield in such circumstances: indeed, in some instances, the nation concerned had no practical power to control the flow of humanity.

Refugee law was designed to effect a compromise between the reality of this largely unstoppable flow of involuntary migrants across European borders and the broader policy commitment to restrictionism in immigration. At least in its initial form, refugee law constituted a humanitarian exception to the protectionist norm,' in that immigration screening was dispensed with for large groups of unprotected migrants.

From 1920 until 1935, refugees were defined in largely juridical terms, which meant that they were treated as refugees because of their membership in a group of persons effectively deprived of the formal protection of the government of its state of origin. The purpose of refugee status conceived in juridical terms is to facilitate the international movement of persons who find themselves abroad and unable to resettle because no nation is prepared to assume responsibility for them. These first refugee definitions were formulated in response to the international legal dilemma caused by the denial of state protection. The withdrawal of dejure protection by a state, whether by way of denaturalisation or the withholding of diplomatic facilities such as travel documents and consular representation, results in a malfunction in the international legal system.

Because the then existing international law did not recognise individuals as subjects of international rights and obligations, the determination of responsibilities on the international plane fell to the sovereign state whose protection one enjoyed. When the bond of protection between citizen and state was severed, no international entity could be held accountable for the individual's actions.

The result was that states were reluctant to admit to their territory individuals who were not the legal responsibility of another country. The refugee definitions adopted between 1920 and 1935 were designed to correct this breakdown, in the international order, and accordingly embraced persons who wished to have freedom of international movement but found themselves in the anomalous situation of not enjoying the legal protection of any state.

The most fundamental form of dejure withdrawal of state protection is, of course, denaturalisation. It was the general policy of the League of Nations to extend protection to groups of persons whose nationality had been involuntarily withdrawn. As well, the League recognised that persons who could not obtain valid passports were entitled to international protection. Both of these groups received League of Nations 'identity certificates which contracting states agreed to recognise as the functional equivalent of passports.

The definitions of this era contained a criterion of ethnic or territorial origin, coupled with a stipulation that the applicant not enjoy dejure national protection . Only persons applying from outside their country of origin were eligible for refugee recognition. This is consistent with the notion of the refugee as an international anomaly: while the unprotected individual remained within the boundaries of her home state, there was no question of another country being confronted with a person outside the bounds of international accountability and, accordingly, no need to include her within the scope of League of Nations protection. In contrast to the initial juridical focus, the refugee agreements adopted between 1935 and 1939 embodied a social approach to refugee definition. Refugees defined from the social perspective are the helpless casualties of broadly based social or political occurrences which separate them from their home society.

Assistance in migration is afforded refugees not, as from the juridical perspective, with a view to correcting an anomaly in the international legal system, but rather in order to ensure the refugees' safety or well-being. The categories of persons eligible for international assistance encompassed groups adversely affected by a particular social or political event, not just those united by a common status vis-a-vis the international legal system. The essence of this second definitional approach was to continue to assist persons without formal national legal protection, but to assist as well the victims of social and political events which resulted in a defacto, if not a dejure, loss of state protection. For the most part, these agreements sought to protect persons caught up in the upheaval and dislocation caused by the National Socialist regime in Germany. The substantive scope of this era's definitions was defined by an en bloc reference to general, situation-specific categories of persons affected by adverse social or political phenomena.

The third phase of international refugee protection, comprising the accords of the 1938-1950 era, was revolutionary in its rejection of group determination of refugee status. A refugee by individualist standards is a person in search of an escape from perceived injustice or fundamental incompatibility with her home state. She distrusts the authorities who have rendered continued residence in her country of origin either impossible or intolerable, and desires the opportunity to build a new life abroad.

Refugee status viewed from this perspective is a means of facilitating international movement for those in search of personal freedom. This individualist approach first affected the determination procedure: the decision as to whether or not a person was a refugee was no longer made strictly on the basis of political and social categories. Rather, the accords of the immediate post-war era prescribed an examination of the merits of each applicant's case. Moreover, the move to a more personal conception of refugee hood altered substantive notions. The essence of refugee status came to be discord between the individual refugee applicant's personal characteristics and convictions and the tenets of the political system in her country of origin. The subjective concept of a refugee was not universally embraced by the international community.

During debate in the United Nations in 1946, for example, the socialist states asserted the impropriety of including political dissidents among the ranks of refugees protected by international law. It was argued unsuccessfully that political emigres who had suffered no personal prejudice ought not be protected as refugees under the auspices of the international community as a whole, but should instead seek the assistance of those states sympathetic to their political views." The voting strength and influence of the Western alliance, however, led to a movement away from a focus on group de jure or de facto disfranchisement, and toward a personalized evaluation of incompatibility between state of origin and refugee claimant in search of personal freedom and liberty. This initiative to define the refugee concept in a manner consistent with the ideology of the more powerful states set the stage for the development of contemporary international refugee law.

The primary standard of refugee status today is that derived from the 1951 Convention relating to the Status of Refugees. In addition to continuing protection for all persons deemed to be refugees under any of the earlier international accords, the mandate of the Convention includes any person who ... as a result of events occurring before 1 January 1951 and owing to well-founded fear of being persecuted for reasons of race, religion, nationality, membership of a particular social group or political opinion, is outside the country of his nationality and is unable or, owing to such fear, is unwilling to avail himself of the protection of that country; or who, not having a nationality and being outside the country of his former habitual residence as a result of such events, is unable or, owing to such fear, is unwilling to return to it.

Provisions dealing with dual or multiple nationality and the circumstances in which one may either cease to be a refugee or be excluded from the benefits of refugee status are also set out. The Convention was drafted between 1948 and 1951 by a combination of United Nations organs, ad hoc committees, and a conference of plenipotentiaries. The two main characteristics of the Convention refugee definition are its strategic conceptualization and its Eurocentric focus. The strategic dimension of the definition comes from successful efforts of Western states to give priority in protection matters to persons whose flight was motivated by pro-Western political values.

As anxious as the Soviets had been to exclude political emigres from the scope of the Convention for fear of exposing their weak flank, so the more numerous and more powerful Western states were preoccupied to maximize the international visibility of that migration. In the result, it was agreed to restrict the scope of protection in much the same way as had been done in the post-World War II refugee instruments: only persons who feared "persecution" because of their civil or political status would fall within the international protection mandate. This apparently neutral formulation facilitated the condemnation of Soviet bloc politics through international law in two ways. First, the persecution standard was a known quantity, having already been employed to embrace

Soviet bloc dissidents in the immediate post-war years. It was understood that the concept of persecution" was sufficiently open-ended to allow the West to continue to admit ideological dissidents to international protection. Second, the precise formulation of the persecution standard meant that refugee law could not readily be turned to the political advantage of the Soviet bloc. The refugee definition was carefully phrased to include only persons who have been disfranchised by their state on the basis of race, religion, nationality, membership of a particular social group; or political opinion, matters in regard to which East bloc practice has historically been problematic.

Western vulnerability in the area of respect for human rights, in contrast, centres more on the guarantee of socio-economic human rights than on respect for civil and political rights. Unlike the victims of civil and political oppression, however, persons denied even such basic rights as food, health care, or education are excluded from the international refugee regime (unless that deprivation stems from civil or political status). By mandating protection for those whose (Western inspired) civil and political rights are jeopardized, without at the same time protecting persons whose (socialist inspired) socio-economic rights are at risk, the Convention adopted an incomplete and politically partisan human rights rationale. The 1967 Protocol achieved the formal, but not the substantive, universalization of the Convention definition of refugee status. The obvious restriction in the Convention definition - the requirement that the claim relate to a pre-1951 event in Europe - was prospectively eliminated by the Protocol. However, there was no review conducted of the substantive content of the definition.

Even after the elimination of temporal and geographic limitations, only persons whose migration is prompted by a fear of persecution on the ground of civil or political status come within the scope of the Convention-based protection system. This means that most Third World refugees remain de facto excluded, as their flight *is* more often prompted by natural' disaster, war, or broadly based political and economic turmoil than by "persecution", at least as that term is understood in the Western context. While these phenomena undoubtedly may give rise to genuine fear and hence to the need to seek safe haven away from one's home, refugees whose flight is not motivated by persecution rooted in civil or political status are excluded from the rights regime established by the Convention.

The Convention refugee concept has been expanded in practice through the evolution of the institutional competence of the United Nations High Commissioner for Refugees, the effort to prepare a United Nations convention on territorial asylum, the establishment of regional refugee protection arrangements, and the practice of states. While these developments do not constitute formal amendments to the Convention definition, they are nonetheless indicative of a widening of the circumstances in which persons may be said genuinely to be in need of international protection. In keeping with Recommendation E of the Conference that adopted the Convention, states which are parties to the Convention may be expected to consider these developments in determining the extent to which persons outside the strict contractual scope of the Convention will be protected as refugees.

Developments in the refugee definition employed by the United Nations High Commissioner for Refugees are salient particularly because this institutional definition and the Convention definition were drafted simultaneously by the same organs of the United Nations. Since the adoption of the 1967 Protocol, moreover, the two definitions are quite similar. The individualistic character of the refugee definition contained in the 1950 UNHCR Statute made it difficult initially for the organization to respond in a meaningful way to the needs of refugees outside Europe. Because refugees in Africa and Asia tend to move in large groups, the type of individuated, case by case application of a refugee definition contemplated by the Statute (like the Convention) was simply not a practical possibility.

The UNHCR was thus technically unable to exercise its universal mandate, and sought the authority to deal with refugee situations outside Europe in a more collective fashion that would not involve a process of individualized assessment. Since 1957, the General Assembly, the Economic and Social Council, and the Executive Committee of the UNHCR have moved by a variety of means to respond to non-European refugee-producing situations. Styled variously as requests for the UNHCR to "extend its good offices", or to act on behalf of groups "of concern" to the international community, the defacto sphere of responsibility has expanded radically from its relatively constrained statutory base. UNHCR has been authorized to aid the full range of involuntary migrants, including the victims of all forms of both man-made and natural disasters.

Moreover, the organization has been requested to assist refugees who remain within their country of origin, and to contribute to the resettlement of refugees who are returning home. The essential criterion of refugee status under UNHCR auspices has come to be simply the existence of human suffering consequent to forced migration. While this enhanced definition is linked primarily to eligibility for material assistance, UNHCR has also been authorized with increasing frequency to extend international legal protection to persons within its broader mandate. In functional terms, few distinctions are now made between the role of UNHCR in regard to refugees within its statutory mandate and those within its extended competence.

A second indication of the expanded scope of refugee status derives from the abortive effort to draft a convention to define the circumstances in which territorial asylum should be guaranteed to refugees. The need for such a convention stems from the failure to include in the Convention any obligation beyond "non-refoulement", that is, the duty to avoid the return of a refugee to a country where she faces a genuine risk of serious harm. While willing to provide emergency protection against return to persecution the states that participated in the drafting of the Convention insisted that they be allowed to decide who should be admitted to their territory, who should be allowed to remain there, and ultimately who should be permanently resettled. In view of this deficiency in the Convention, and in an, effort to effectuate the right to seek and enjoy asylum contained in the Universal Declaration of Human Rights and the Declaration on Territorial Asylum, a draft convention on territorial asylum was prepared and submitted to a conference of plenipotentiaries in 1977.

While the purpose of the proposed accord was essentially to enhance the scope of protection available to Convention refugees, its most noteworthy achievement may in fact have been the degree of consensus attained on changes to the definition of refugee status for purposes of entitlement to international legal protection. The expert draft of Article 2 of the proposed asylum convention recommended important changes to the definitional standard derived from the Convention, as amended by the Protocol. Clarifications of the notions of (4 political opinion" to include opposition to apartheid and colonialism, and of "persecution" to embrace prosecution grounded in persecutory intent were proposed. During the meeting of the 92 states, moreover, it was agreed inter alia that asylum should be accessible also to persons at serious risk of persecution due to kinship or as a result of "foreign occupation, alien domination, and all forms of racism." An important clarification of the definition agreed to by delegates was the replacement of the "owing to a well-founded fear of persecution" Convention-based standard with a requirement that a refugee be "faced with a definite possibility of persecution." The expanded scope of protection as a whole, including both the expert group and conference amendments, which was approved by 47 votes to 14 with 21 abstentions, provided that:

> Each Contracting state may grant the benefits of this Convention to a person seeking asylum, if he, being faced with a definite possibility of:
>
> (a) Persecution for reasons of race, colour, national or ethnic origin, religion, nationality, kinship, membership of a particular social group or political opinion, including the struggle against colonialism and apartheid, foreign occupation, alien domination and all forms of racism; or
>
> (b) Prosecution or punishment for reasons directly related to the persecution set forth in (a);
>
> is unable or unwilling to return to the country of his nationality or, if he has no nationality, the country of his former domicile or habitual residence.

While the drafting of the territorial asylum convention ended in a stalemate, the affirmative vote in favour of an expanded definition of refugee status is nonetheless indicative of a willingness on the part of the international community to conceive the refugee concept more broadly than as elaborated in the Convention and Protocol. In contrast to the concern in 1967 to avoid the reassessment of the substantive content of the refugee definition, a majority of the 92 states that attended the Conference on Territorial Asylum agreed to update the definition in ways that were responsive to refugee movements in the developing world, and which recognized the collective nature of many refugee-producing phenomena. While no binding, conventional commitment was established toward refugees within this revised concept, the work of the 1977 conference remains the most recent expression of international consensus on the appropriate scope of refugee status in international law. Three regional groups have enacted standards of refugee protection that extend the Convention definition in ways similar to the evolution of the UNHCR mandate and the scope of the proposed asylum convention. The work of each of the Organization of African Unity, the Organization of American States, and the Council of Europe is considered in turn.

In the present volume, we have made an attempt to address the cause of refugee population in the world and many relevant mandatory provisions for the protection of their basic human rights are also dealt with ebborately.

First we shall take up the concept of refugee in the context of international law.

2

Refugee Concept in International Law

> "What can be more foolish than to think that all this rare fabric of heaven and earth could come by chance, when all the skill of science is not able to make an oyster."
>
> —*Jeremy Taylor*

Taking into account the consensus on the extension of the mandate of the UNHCR, the agreement reached on broadening the refugee concept at the Conference on Territorial Asylum, the conceptual advances of the three regional refugee accords, and the consequent, shifts in the practice of states, can it be said that modern international law recognizes any duty toward a class of refugees more broad than as defined in the Convention and Protocol?

Guy Goodwin-Gill has argued that a new class of refugees is recognized in customary international law. He believes that the obligation of states to observe the principle of "non-refoulement", implying at least temporary refuge in the face of imminent danger, now extends to persons outside the Convention refugee definition insofar as they may be said to lack governmental protection against harmful events beyond their choosing or control. Persons who flee situations of civil disorder, domestic conflict, or human rights violations should benefit from a presumption of humanitarian need, and may not be returned unless the state of refuge can rebut the presumed risk of danger.

On the other hand, Kay Hailbronner characterizes such views as "wishful legal thinking" on the basis that there is neither extensive and uniform state practice nor opinio juris sufficient to warrant an assertion of international rights for refugees outside the scope of the Convention. Hailbronner notes that most of the international practice in favour of the expanded class of refugees is in fact UNHCR institutional practice, which cannot be said to bind states in their own actions. Moreover, regional standards, have not been codified in binding terms, and national efforts on behalf of humanitarian refugees have been carefully defined as discretionary exercises of prerogative over immigration.

In so far as there is an international legal consensus on an expanded conceptualization of refugee status based upon custom, it surely is, as Goodwin-Gill concedes, "at a relatively low level of commitment." In my view, Goodwill-Gill's assertion of a right to protection against "refoulement" overstates the extant scope of customary law in regard to non-Convention refugees.

As noted by Hailbronner, developed states have felt free to reject members of the broader class of asylum seekers by the imposition of visa requirements, penalties on transportation companies, naval blockades, and the establishment of strictly discretionary mechanisms to cope with those asylum seekers who do reach their territory. Developing states have conditioned their willingness to protect humanitarian refugees on the agreement of the international community to underwrite the costs of temporary asylum and to relocate the refugees to states of permanent resettlement.

Even the UNHCR has been tentative in its assertion of an expanded scope for the refugee definition applicable in the context of legal protection decisions. On the other hand, Hailbronner overlooks the consensus at the global, regional, and national levels in favour of addressing in some way the claims of those persons in one's territory or at one's borders who fear harm in their country of origin as a result of serious disturbances of public order. No aspect of international practice has questioned the duty to examine their need for protection. The nature of the special consideration has varied, and the avoidance of "refoulement" has not been universal. Nonetheless, UNHCR practice, the international consensus at the, Conference on Territorial Asylum, all three regional refugee accords, and, relatively consistent state practice agree in their extension of some opportunity for special consideration to persons within a state's territory who have been victimized by serious disturbances of public order in their country of origin.

The level of commitment is lower than that suggested by Goodwin-Gill, but an intermediate category of refugee protection does now exist. The customary norm rooted in international usage is a right to be considered for temporary admission, whether by formal procedure or administrative discretion, on the basis of a need for protection. That is, customary international law precludes the making of decisions to reject or expel persons who come from nations in which there are serious disturbances of public order without-explicit attention being paid to their humanitarian needs. This duty may be met through the granting of formal status as is contemplated by the three regional refugee accords, through the discretionary programs of "B" status, special measures, or extended voluntary departure that exist in Western developed state, or by seeking the assistance of other states or the international community to share the burden of actual or impending refugee flows.

The obligation is simply to do something which provides a meaningful response to the humanitarian needs of the victims of serious disruptions of public order. We have not yet reached the point, though, of assimilating such persons to Convention refugees for the purpose of stipulating a duty to avert return in all cases.

In sum, international law may be said to recognize four categories of refugees. First are refugees defined by the Convention and Protocol. Convention refugees are entitled to claim protection against return to a country in which they fear persecution from any of the more than one hundred state parties to these accords. They may also invoke the full range of rights set out in the Convention, and call upon the institutional support of the UNHCR. Second, there are refugees who are protected by a regional agreement. Such persons may be at risk of return to, a situation of serious disturbance of public order, rather than persecution.

Nonetheless, at least within Africa and Latin America, they are generally protected against return, and 'may be entitled to other preferential rights akin to those afforded Convention refugees. Third, there are refugees who fear harm as a result of serious disturbances of public order, but who are not able to invoke the protection of a special regional arrangement.

These refugees from man-made harm are entitled to special consideration prior to return to their state of origin, but they may not claim protection from return as of right except as stipulated in the national legislation of the asylum state. Finally, all persons who are involuntary migrants as a result of natural or man-made causes may claim the institutional support of UNHCR by way of material assistance, aid in voluntary repatriation or resettlement, and in some cases legal protection. This residual class of refugees, however, has no special claim to protection under international law.

Thus, the refugee definition is an inevitable starting point in all refugee law discussions. It is therefore not surprising that it should have been the subject of Article I of the Bangkok Principles. This is of the utmost importance in that it is necessary to provide predictable and fair criteria by which to distinguish refugees from migrants. The refugee definition has the further advantage of succinctly calling attention to the essential problem of the refugee and highlighting his/her central needs. While the definition in the Bangkok Principles is generally consistent with that of the 1.951 Convention relating to the Status of Refugees, the 30th anniversary year of the Bangkok Principles provides an opportunity to re-examine it in light of universal and regional developments in refugee law and of the practice of States in Asia and Africa, An agreed refugee definition is among other things, a way of making clear the distinction between refugees and migrants.

The latter, like refugees, cross borders in a regular or irregular manner, but with the difference that they have no need for the protection of international refugee law. It is therefore a way to ensure that those who are in need of international protection have access to it. By the same token it helps ensuring that those who do not need or deserve international protection do not abuse the humanitarian institution of asylum, and that the efforts of the international community in this field are concentrated on those who are really of concern, In this context, the refugee definition underlines the need to guarantee this particularly vulnerable population the exercise of the right to seek and enjoy asylum from persecution and the effective implementation of the basic principles of refugee protection.

The definition also provides predictable and fair criteria governing the grant of refugee status. Further more it, emphasizes the responsibility of the international community for the protection and humanitarian assistance of persons fleeing persecution, thereby creating one of the conditions for the operation of the principle of international solidarity and burden-sharing. The refugee problem has been considered a matter of global international concern since 1921 under the League of Nations. In the post-Cold-War world, this is more necessary as the refugee problem has grown in magnitude and complexity. An agreed and widely implemented definition constitutes an objective basis for international cooperation in solving the refugee problem. The launching of prevention' policies as well as of solution-oriented strategies firstly depends on an understanding on whom the effective involvement of the international community should be directed to.

Under Article -1 of the Principles concerning the Treatment of Refugees a refugee is defined as:

> a person who, owing to persecution or well-founded fear of persecution for reasons of race, colour, religion, political belief or membership of a particular social group

(a) leaves the State of which he is a national or the country of his nationality, or, if he has no nationality, the State or the Country of which is a habitual resident or

(b) being outside such State or Country, is unable or unwilling to return to it or to avail himself of its protection.

To be recognised as a refugee, the applicant must fulfil two basic conditions, which relate to being outside the country of nationality or, for stateless persons, of the country of habitual residence, and to being unable or unwilling to return to it or to avail oneself of the protection of that country. The claim must furthermore be based on a particular reason, i.e. race, colour, religion, political belief or membership in a particular social group. The meaning of the concept of persecution is not defined by the Bangkok Principles, or by any other international instrument concerning refugees, however, The well-founded tear of being persecuted constitutes the central element of this definition, as for that of the 1951 Convention. It is traditionally considered as including two basic components reflecting the subjective and objective aspects of the refugee condition. The subjective element relates to the fear of being persecuted. Fear is, by definition, a state of mind which depends on the personality of the applicant, as well as on his/her culture-social experience, family and personal backgrounds.

It determines the interpretation the concerned person makes of his/her personal situation, As regards the objective aspect of the refugee definition, i.e., the well foundedness of the claim, the applicant's credibility must be assessed by objective elements corroborating the fear of persecution. The possession of up- to-date and reliable information on the situation in the country of origin is essential, but it does not imply a value judgement on, or interference in, the internal affairs of that country. After all, refugee protection is a humanitarian and non-political matter, The assessment of an eventual future risk of persecution takes place at the time of the making of the decision.

Past persecution is not required, although acts of persecution or denials of human rights prior to the flight can create a presumption of future persecution, as long as the basic circumstances have not changed. The grounds of the persecution may relate either to the claimant's activities prior or subsequent to his/tier flight, or they may be a consequence of the departure itself or of the prolonged absence that followed. It may also be a consequence of a political change in the country of origin, or of a change of views on the part of the claimant, while the latter was already abroad.

Regarding the agent of persecution, the persecutor may be the State or a non-State actor, in the latter case when the State either directly or indirectly tolerates or encourages the wrongful acts, or simply fails to assume its obligation of protection towards its citizens, The persecuted may be threatened individually or as a member of a particular cultural, religious, social, or political group. This definition obviously excludes from international protection the victims of natural disasters, as well as the persons who leave their country for personal reasons, either to work or to improve their standard of living, known as "migrants" or "economic migrants".

The refugee definition contained in the Bangkok Principles is to that of Article I of the 1951 Convention relating to the Status of Refugees'. By avoiding the geographical and temporal limitations contained in the 1951 Convention, however, the Bangkok Principles foreshadowed the 1967 Protocol relating to the Status of Refugees. Nevertheless, there are some differences between the Bangkok Principles' refugee definition and those of other international instruments. As far as possible, a minimal homogenisation of the international norms would simplify the use of these instruments and consequently improve the actual protection of refugees. The inclusion of the term "nationality" as a ground of persecution or fear of persecution for a person to qualify as a refugee would bring this definition closer to those of other instruments. Similarly, the concept of "refugee sur place" contained in paragraph (vi) of the Notes to Article 1, which provides for "a person who was outside of the State of which he is a national or the Country of his nationality, or if he has no nationality the State of the country of which he is habitual resident, at the time of the events which caused him to have a well founded fear of above mentioned persecution and is unable or unwilling to return to it or to avail himself of its protection shall be considered a refugee", could be considered for inclusion in the definition itself.

It is appropriate, in light of developments in the region as well as in other parts of the world over the last thirty years, to consider further the issue of the scope of the definition under the Bangkok Principles. The adoption of an expanded refugee definition would put the Bangkok Principles in line with the actual practice of the Member States. It is significant that one paragraph of the Notes to Article I of the Bangkok Principles hints at a broader definition for the Asian-African region. Indeed, in paragraph (ii) of the Notes, three Delegations proposed that "the definition of the term 'refugee' include a person who is obliged to leave the State of which he is a national under the pressure of an illegal act or as a result of invasion of such State, wholly or partially, by an alien with a view to occupying the State".

This view anticipates the 1969 OAU Convention in which a purportedly broader definition includes that of the 1951 Convention, but extends it in order to take account of the specific regional aspects of the refugee problem in Africa. The OAU Convention definition indeed covers, in addition to persons with a well founded fear of persecution on the grounds specified in the 1951 Convention, "every person who, owing to external aggression, occupation, foreign domination, or events seriously disturbing public order in either part or the whole of his country of origin or nationality, is compelled to leave his place of habitual residence in order to seek refuge in another place outside his country of origin or nationality". The importance and timeliness of this ground-breaking initiative was acknowledged and echoed by the AALCC as early as 1970 when it adopted the first Addendum to the Principles concerning Treatment of Refugees at its 11th Session in New Delhi. The Addendum opened indeed by stating in its preamble:

> "Whereas it appears to the Committee on further consideration that the Principles adopted at its Session in Bangkok in 1966 mainly contemplated the status of what may be called political refugees who have been deprived of the protection of their own Government and do not provide adequately for the case of other refugees and displaced persons.

And whereas the Committee considers that such other refugees or displaced persons should enjoy the benefit of protection of the nature afforded by Articles IV and V of those Principles." The AALCC was referring of course to the right to return and the right to compensation which are the subjects of the first Addendum. The Addendum went on to spell out in its first paragraph who those other refugees and displaced persons are who should enjoy these rights, as follows:

> "Any person who because of foreign domination, external aggression or occupation has left his habitual place of residence, or being outside such place desires to return thereto but is prevented from doing so by the Government or authorities in control of such place of his habitual residence from which he was displaced."

While this formulation addresses specifically the issue of

return and compensation and furthermore does not explicitly differentiate between refugees and displaced persons, it is clearly a reflection 'and acknowledgement of the OAU Convention definition. In the context of the Central American refugee problem, Latin American countries took an approach similar to that of the OAU Convention in the 1984 Cartagena Declaration which recommends that the refugee definition should include, in order to meet the special needs of the Latin American region, persons who have, fled a situation of "generalized violence, foreign aggression, internal conflicts, massive violations of human rights or other circumstances which have seriously disturbed public order." The Cartagena Declaration was endorsed by the General Assembly of the Organisation of American States (OAS) and the States of the region have incorporated the enlarged definition into their domestic legislation.

Later on, this definition was reaffirmed and extended by the 1994 San Jose Declaration, adopted in commemoration of the 10th anniversary of the Cartagena Declaration. The refugee definitions contained in the OAU Convention and the Cartagena Declaration (Annex) aim at providing international protection to persons fleeing a situation of civil or international war. They take account of the particular characteristics of the refugee flows in the regions concerned. Indeed, while the 1951 Convention definition includes a subjective component relating to the individual fear of being persecuted, the enlarged definitions in the above mentioned regional instruments call for consideration of the objective situation in the country of origin and of the needs of protection and assistance of persons concerned, who, not necessarily being faced with individual acts of persecution, do not meet the conditions of the 1951 Convention.

The different grounds on which a person may be entitled

to claim international protection under the enlarged definition reflect the fact that the domestic or international conflicts faced by the concerned States are at the origin of most of the international displacements which take place in these regions. Responding to the development and diversification of the domestic and international conflicts, and to the intensification of forced population displacements, these regions initiated the process of improvement of the existing instruments of international protection. While in Africa these concerns have been translated into a binding international instrument, they have been firmly reflected in the practice of both Africa and Asia.

The definitions in these regional instruments include several grounds for a person or group of persons to qualify as refugees. "Generalized violence" would result from armed civil or international conflicts, and must be continuous and sustained, which distinguishes generalized violence from momentary tensions. Generalized violence might cover two situations: internal conflict and foreign aggression. The latter, which may include "external aggression, occupation or foreign domination", refers to a dispute between two States leading to the use of armed force by a State against the territorial integrity of another State. "Massive violations of human rights" would consist in large-scale violations of basic rights as stated in the relevant international instruments.

The "other circumstances which have seriously disturbed the public order", or "events seriously disturbing public order in either part or the whole of the country" would be the result of human actions based on social, economic, political or ideological, conflicts. The practice of African and Asian States widely confirms that the refugee definition as stated in the above mentioned instruments, is a manifestation of a need of the international community in this field.

Indeed such definitions have proved particularly useful. They reflect the fact that civil and international conflicts are at the origin of most refugee flows.

In the years since the adoption of the Bangkok Principles, the Asian countries generously granted admission to large numbers of refugees. They were thus able to tackle the large flows of population seeking asylum which Asia has been faced with since the early seventies. This record, which is chronicled in the Background Note, underlines the relevance of a refugee definition which encompasses both persons with a well-founded fear of persecution and the victims of large-scale international or civil violence. The practice of the United Nations also highlights the interest of such an enlarged definition. Indeed, the General Assembly has on several occasions adopted Resolutions requesting the High Commissioner to extend his/her good offices to specific groups of refugees not covered by the narrower definition, the cumulative effect of which has been to legitimise an expanded definition.

The expanded definition would contribute to strengthening the international regime of refugee protection by matching principles with the practice of States in Asia and, by extending to that region, even if on a non-binding basis, the agreed principles already adopted in Africa and in Latin America, and endorsed by the United Nations General Assembly.

Like the 1951 Convention and the OAU Convention, the Bangkok Principles also specify certain circumstances under which refugee status does not apply. Exclusion clauses provide that refugee status shall not apply to persons who meet the inclusion criteria, but who nevertheless do not need or deserve international protection.

Those listed under *"Exceptions"* in Article I (I) and (2) of the Bangkok Principles exclude persons who can avail themselves of the protection of another State or Country in cases of multiple nationality. The Bangkok Principles also exclude as undeserving of international protection, persons responsible for crimes against peace, war crimes, crimes against humanity, serious non-political crimes., or acts contrary to the purposes and principles of the United Nations. Both the 1951 Convention (Article 1 [F] [a]) and the OAU Convention (Article 1 [5] [a]) clarify that the crimes against peace, war crimes and crimes against humanity which they refer to are those "defined in international instruments drawn up to make provisions for such crimes". Among these, Article 6 of the Charter of the International Military Tribunal (Nuremberg Tribunal) provides useful '-definitions" of these crimes.

The Statutes of the International Criminal Tribunals for the Former Yugoslavia and for Rwanda are also relevant in this respect. The 1951 Convention and OAU Convention further specify that the "serious non.-political crime" referred to in their Articles I F (b) and 1 (5) (b) must have been "committed outside the country of refuge prior to his admission to that country as a refugee". Otherwise, it *is* not an exclusion issue, but one related, to the application of the criminal justice system of the country of refuge. If expulsion or deportation were envisaged in such a case, it would be considered, as appropriate, under Articles 111 (3) and VIII of the Bangkok Principles, Article 11 (3) of the OAU Convention, or Articles 32 and 33 of the 1951 Convention, which deal with expulsion and non-refoulement. Additionally, the OAU Convention covers such matters under its cessation clauses (Article 1 [4] [f] and [g]). Furthermore, it is important to note, with respect to exclusion clauses, that they are strictly limitative and therefore other causes cannot be invoked on an ad hoc basis to deny refugee status to a person who otherwise qualifies.

First it is significant to note that refugees are at risk of human rights violations in their home country. The work UNHCR does to ensure they are not subject to refoulement is a direct and powerful means of protecting their basic human rights, In the last decade, refugees who have been forcibly returned to their countries have been killed, tortured, arbitrarily detained, or forced to live in conditions of extreme insecurity. Preventing refoulement is an effective, and sometimes the only, means of preventing further human rights violations.

Those who flee their own countries in search of protection abroad do so precisely because their human rights are at risk in their own country. To decide that an individual has a "well-founded fear of persecution" is in effect to conclude that one or more of his or her basic human rights are not being respected.

Similarly, to determine that a group of people fleeing conflict or serious disturbances of the public order are prima facie refugees is in most cases to acknowledge that they are victims of violations of human rights or humanitarian law. If conditions have fundamentally changed in the country of origin, promoting and monitoring the safety of their voluntary return allows refugees to re-establish themselves in their own community and to enjoy their basic human rights. In addition, monitoring the safety of returnees is a means of ensuring that they do not again suffer the human rights violations which forced them to flee.

In a relatively small number of cases, assisting refugees to be integrated locally or resettled in another country is a means of ensuring that refugees who cannot return to their own countries are able to find a new home where they can take up residence and enjoy a secure legal status and basic human rights. UNHCR staff undertake activities such as these on a daily basis in countries around the world, meaning that UNHCR is perhaps the largest operational UN human rights agency.

As the High Commissioner for Refugees explained in her statement to the 50th session of the UN Commission on Human Rights (1994):

> "The connection between the work of the Commission in promoting respect for human rights and the work of my Office, in protecting refugees and seeking solutions to refugee problems is clear. As I mentioned in my address to the Commission last year, human rights violations are a major factor in causing the flight of refugees as well as an obstacle to their safe and voluntary return home. Safeguarding human rights in countries of origin is therefore critical both for the prevention and for the solution of refugee problems. Respect for human rights is also essential for the protection of refugees in countries of asylum".

No doubt UNHCR's core functions involve protecting human rights, not everyone is accustomed to thinking of the Office as a "human rights" organization. Most UNHCR staff have not been involved on a systematic basis in the promotion or use of international human rights standards, Three recurring questions frequently come up when discussing incorporating human rights law more consistently into UNHCR's protection activities,

Beginning with the Statute of the Office, UNHCR's mandate has been described as a humanitarian one, meaning that actions in favour of refugees should be non-partisan and non-political with the sole concern being the safety and welfare of the refugees. This understanding of refugee protection as humanitarian work allows countries of asylum to respond to the needs of refugees without passing judgment on the country of origin, which is often a neighbouring state, while the acceptance of UNHCR as a humanitarian agency helps to ensure support for our work. Placing greater reliance on human rights standards as a basis for UNHCR's work does not jeopardize the humanitarian character of our activities, since international human rights law is itself non-political and non-partisan.

- international human rights law treats all countries equally by imposing the same standards and obligations on each state regardless of the ideology of any particular government; and
- many provisions of international human rights law have been universally accepted and/or specifically undertaken by states, and advocating their implementation is not apolitical" but simply asking governments to live up to their obligations,

Of course, the debate surrounding human rights can become politicised and controversial. Different governments or organizations opposed to particular governments may use the language of human rights to advance particular policies which may or may not in fact be supported by reference to human rights law. Also, governments may be inclined to use human rights law selectively, either by criticizing the human rights record of rival governments while remaining silent regarding friendly governments, or by emphasizing only certain aspects of their own human rights records. However, many UNHCR staff are accustomed to having their work helped or hindered by different governments or political groupings — this does not stop

UNHCR from insisting on its responsibility to provide international protection to refugees. It does mean however, that UNHCR must ensure its work is non-partisan:

- by being consistent in the rights it defends; and
- by defending those rights in all circumstances regardless of the politics of the refugee or the country concerned.

As such, if UNHCR staff ensure that they use human rights law impartially, then the humanitarian and non-political nature of our work is not threatened. Some people believe that the international "law" of human rights is not really law at all but simply a set of noble aspirations describing an ideal world which has little relation to reality.

Those who work with refugees maybe particularly tempted to hold such a view, since the growing number of refugees in the world is apparent proof of the failure of the system of international human rights protection. It is true that even the most basic human rights are routinely violated, and that efforts by international, bodies to ensure respect for human rights are often fruitless. However, this does not mean that international human rights law is of no use to UNHCR but simply that it has limitations. The difficulties of enforcing international human rights law are similar to the difficulties of enforcing most branches of international law. Like many human rights treaties, the 1951 Convention is not always honoured by states parties - but it continues to be of real help to countless numbers of individuals who rely on its provisions and UNHCR continues to insist on respect for the principles it establishes. As a UN agency, UNHCR has a duty to promote the purposes of the UN, including the protection of human rights, of UN Charter Art 1.3. Greater reliance by UNHCR on international human rights law will contribute to greater respect for and more effective implementation of this law.

International human rights law is more complex than international refugee law, because of the multiplicity of sources and standards compared to the few refugee law instruments whose provisions are relatively straightforward. In addition, there are dozens of human rights issues that are in one way or another the subject of UN attention. For non-specialists, this can be bewildering or frustrating. However, despite these difficulties there do exist certain core standards which have been universally accepted. Many of them have been elaborated in binding legal instruments to which a majority of states are party. More importantly, it does not require a specialist knowledge of the whole body of international human rights law in order to rely on some of it to protect the rights of refugees.

In fact, the most basic right for refugees is the right not to be subject to refoulement, which is set out in Article 33 of the 1951 Convention. But the 1951 Convention is not the only international treaty which provides protection against refoulement. Similarly, other rights provided for by refugee law, such as non-discrimination, are found in international human rights instruments. Moreover, many refugee protection standards are set out in non-binding conclusions of UNHCR's Executive Committee.

In the next chapter we shall address the responsibilities and concerns of United Nations High Commissioner for Refugees.

3

UNHCR: Responsibilities and Concern

> "For every grain of wit there is a grain of folly. For everything you have missed, you have gained something else; and for everything you gain, you lose something. ... If the gatherer gathers too much, nature takes out of the man what she puts into his chest; swells the estate, but kills the owner. Nature hates monopolies and exceptions."

The United Nations High Commissioner for Refugees, acting under the authority of the General Assembly, shall assume the function of providing international protection, under the auspices of the-United Nations, to refugees who fall within the scope of the present Statute and of seeking permanent solutions for the problem of refugees by assisting Governments and, subject to the approval of the Governments concerned private organizations to facilitate the voluntary repatriation of such refugees or their assimilation within new national communities.

In the exercise of his functions more particularly when difficulties arise, and for instance with regard to any controversy concerning the international status of these persons, the High Commissioner shall request the opinion of the advisory committee on refugees if it is created. The work of the High Commissioner shall be of an entirely non-political character; it shall be humanitarian and social and shall relate, as a rule, to groups and categories of refugees.

The High Commissioner shall follow policy directives given him by the General Assembly or the Economic and Social Council.

The Economic and Social Council may decide, after hearing the views of the High Commissioner on the subject, to establish an advisory committee on refugees which shall consist of representatives of States Members and States non-members of the United Nations, to be selected by the Council on the basis of their demonstrated interest in and devotion to the solution of the refugee problem.

The General Assembly shall review, not later than at its eighth regular Session the arrangements for the Office of the High Commissioner with a view to determining whether the Office should be continued beyond 31 December 1953.

Functions of the High Commissioner

The competence of the High Commissioner shall extend to :

(i) Any person who has, been considered a refugee under the Arrangements of 12 May 1926 and of 30 June 1928 or under the Conventions of 28 October 1933 and 10 February 19 38, the Protocol of 14 September 1939 or the Constitution of the International Refugee Organization.

(ii) Any person who as a result of events occurring before I January 1951 and owing to well-founded fear of being persecuted for reasons of race, religion, nationality or political opinion is outside the country of his nationality and is unable or owing to such fear or for reasons other than personal convenience, is unwilling to avail himself of the protection of that country, or who, not having a nationality and being outside the country of his former habitual residence, is unable or, owing to such fear or for reasons other than personal convenience, is, unwilling to return to it.

Decisions as to eligibility taken by the International Refugee Organization during the period of its activities shall not prevent the status of refugee being accorded to persons who fulfil the conditions of the present, paragraph;

The competence of the High Commissioner shall cease to apply to any person defined in section A above if:

(a) He has voluntarily reaviled himself of the protection of the country of his nationality; or

(b) Having lost his nationality he has voluntarily reacquired it; or

(c) He has acquired a new nationality and enjoys the protection of the country of his new nationality; or

(d) He has voluntarily re-established himself in the country which he left or outside which he remained owing to fear of persecution; or

(e) He can no longer, because the circumstances in connexion with which he has been recognized as a refugee have ceased to exist, claim grounds other than those of personal convenience for continuing to refuse to avail himself of the protection of the country of his nationality. Reasons of a purely economic character may not be invoked; or

(f) Being a person who has no nationality he can no longer, because the circumstances in connexion with which he has been recognized as a refugee have ceased to exist and he is able to return to the country of his former habitual residence, claim grounds other than those of personal convenience for continuing to refuse to return to that country;

Any other person who is outside the country of his nationality, if he has no nationality, the country of his former habitual residence, because he has or had well-founded fear of persecution by reason of his race, religion, nationality or political opinion and is unable or, because of such fear, is unwilling to avail himself of the protection of the government of the country of his nationality, or, if he has no nationality to return to the country of his former habitual residence.

Provided that the competence of the High Commissioner as defined in paragraph 6 above shall not extend to a person

(a) Who is a national of more than one country unless he satisfies the provisions of the preceding paragraph in relation to each of the countries of which he is a national; or

(b) Who is recognized by the competent authorities of the country in which he has taken residence as having the rights and obligations which are attached to the possession of the nationality of that country; or

(c) Who continues, to receive from other organs or agencies of the United Nations protection or assistance, or-

(d) In respect of whom there are serious reasons for considering that he has committed a crime covered by the provision's of treaties of extradition or a crime mentioned in article VI of the London Charter of the International Military Tribunal or by the provisions of article 14, paragraph 2, of the Universal, Declaration of Human Rights.

The High Commissioner shall provide for the protection of refugees- falling under the competence of his office by :

(a) Promoting the conclusion and ratification of international conventions for the protection of refugees, supervising their application and proposing amendments thereto;

(b) Promoting through special agreements with Governments the execution of any measures calculated to improve the situation of refugees and to reduce the number requiring protection;

(c) Assisting governmental and private efforts to promote voluntary repatriation or assimilation within new national communities;

(d) Promoting the admission of refugees, not excluding those in the most destitute categories, to the territories of States;

(e) Endeavouring to obtain permission for refugees to transfer their assets and especially those necessary for their resettlement;

(f) Obtaining from Governments information concerning the number and conditions of refugees in their territories and the laws and regulations concerning them;

(g) Keeping in close touch with the Governments and inter-governmental organizations concerned;

(h) Establishing contact in such manner as he may think best with private organizations dealing with refugee questions;

(i) Facilitating the co-ordination of the efforts of private organisations concerned with the welfare of refugees.

The High Commissioner shall engage in such additional activities, including repatriation and resettlement as the General Assembly may determine, within the limits of the resources placed at his disposal,

The High Commissioner shall administer any funds. Public or private which he receives for assistance to refugees, and shall distribute them among the private and, as appropriate, public agencies which be deem best qualified to administer such assurance.

The High Commissioner may reject any offers which he does nor consider appropriate or which cannot be utilized.

The High Commissioner shall not appeal to Governments for funds or make a general appeal without, the prior approval of the General Assembly,

The High Commissioner shall include in his annual report a statement of his activities in this field.

The High Commissioner shall he entitled to present his views before the General Assembly, the Economic and Social Council and their subsidiary bodies.

The High Commissioner shall report annually to the General Assembly through the Economic and social council; his report shall, be considered as a separate item on the agenda of the General Assembly,

The High Commissioner may invite the co-operation of the various specialized agencies.

Organization and Finances

The High Commissioner shall be elected by the General

Assembly on the nomination of the Secretary-General. The terms of appointment of the High Commissioner shall be proposed by the Secretary-General and approved by the General Assembly, The High Commissioner shall be elected for a term of three years, from 1 January 1951.

The High Commissioner shall appoint, for the same term, a Deputy High Commissioner of a nationality other than his, own.

(a) Within the limits of the budgetary appropriations provided, the staff of he Office of the High Commissioner shall be appointed by the High Commissioner and shall be responsible to him in the exercise of their functions.

(b) Such staff shall be chosen from persons devoted to the purposes of the Office of the High Commissioner.

(c) Their conditions of employment shall be those provided under the staff regularioas adopted by the General Assembly and the rules promulgated thereunder by the Secretary-General.

(d) Provision May also be made to Permit the employment of personnel without compensation

The High Commissioner shall consult the Government of the countries of residence of refugees as to the need for appointing representatives therein. In any country recognizing such need, there may be appointed a representative approved by the Government of that country. Subject to the foregoing the same representative may serve in more than one country.

The High Commissioner and the Secretary-General shall make appropriate arrangements for liaison and consultation on Matters of mutual interest.

The Secretary-General shall provide the High

Commissioner with all necessary facilities within budgetary limitations.

The Office of the High Commissioner shall be located in Geneva Switzerland.

The Office of the High Commissioner shall be financed under the budget of the United Nations. Unless the General Assembly subsequently decides otherwise, no expenditure other than administrative expenditures relating to the functioning of the Office of the High Commissioner shall be borne on the budget of the United Nations and all other expenditures relating to the activities of the High Commissioner shall be financed by voluntary contributions.

The administration of the Office of the High Commissioner shall be subject to the Financial Regulations of the United Nations and to the financial rules promulgated thereunder by the Secretary General.

Transactions relating to the High Commissioner's funds shall be subject to audit by the United Nations Board of Auditors, provided that the Board may accept audited, accounts from the agencies to which funds, have been allocated. Administrative arrangements for the custody of such, hinds and their allocation shall be agreed between the High Commissioner and the Secretary-General in accordance with the Financial Regulations of the United nations and rules promulgated thereunder by the Secretary General.

A refugee is above all a victim. The 1951 United Nations Convention relating to the Status of Refugees and its 1967 Protocol define a refugee as a person who "owing to well-founded fear of being persecuted for reasons of race, religion, nationality, membership of a particular social group or political opinion, is outside the country of his nationality and is unable or, owing to such fear, is unwilling to avail himself of the protection of that country..."

The word "refugee" in popular usage describes persons in a number of different situations. It is need for example, for persons who are displaced inside a country because of famine or other natural disasters. Such persons are also victims and need help. However, in the international context, the word "refugee" refers to persons who are outside their country of origin and unable or unwilling to return because of a well-founded fear of persecution. UNHCR concern also extends to persons who are compelled to leave their country of origin for other reasons, such as armed conflicts or civil strife, and whose lives or security would be seriously endangered if they returned.

The needs of refugees vary, depending on who and where they are. Their first need is to be protected In many cases, refugees need immediate assistance in the form of food, water, shelter or medical care, But the most fundamental need of a refugee is to be granted asylum. Article 14 of the Universal Declaration of Human Rights states: "Everyone has the right to seek and enjoy in other countries asylum from persecution".

UNHCR is the Office of the United Nations High Commissioner for Refugees. It was created by Resolution 428(y) of the General Assembly of the United Nations, and began its operations on i January 1961. It is a humanitarian and strictly non-political agency devoted to protecting and assisting the world's refugees. In the words of the Statute of the Office, UNHCR has two main functions: to provide "international protection" to refugees and to seek "permanent solutions" for the problems of refugees.

UNHCR had a number of predecessors. To name only a

few: In 1921, the Council of the League of Nations appointed Dr. Fridtjof Nansen "High Commissioner on behalf of the League in connection with the problems of Russian refugees in Europe." In 1931, the League created the International Nansen Office for Refugees and, in 1933, the High Commissioner for Refugees Coming from Germany. In 1943, the United Nations Relief and Rehabilitation Administration was established, and in 1947 the United Nations created the International Refugee Organization.

There are refugees on every continent. In nearly every country around the globe. The only restriction on UNHCR's activity on their behalf in the Office's Statute is the stipulation that the High Commissioner's mandate does not extend to persons who benefit from the protection or assistance of other organs or institutions of the United Nations. One particular case is that of the Palestine refugees. A special organization was set up in 1949 before UNHCR was created-the United Nations Relief and Works Agency for Palestine Refugees in the Near East (UNRWA), which is responsible for providing this group with material assistance, including shelter, food, clothing, health, social services and education. The High Commissioner is elected by the General Assembly of the United Nations on the nomination of the Secretary-General.

Remarkably, UNHCR was initially set up on 1 January 1951 for a period of only three years. The Office is a subsidiary organ of the General Assembly, under Article 22 of the UN Charter, and it depends on the Assembly for renewal of its mandate. The first, time the General Assembly reviewed the need to prolong IJNHCR's mandate was in 1953. Since then, it has been clear that refugee problems require the continued attention of the United Nations, and UNHCR's mandate has been renewed every five years.

UNHCR has representatives accredited to more than 100 countries. Its Headquarters are in Geneva, Switzerland. Nearly 2,000 men and women work for UNHCR. They come from many different countries, but what they have in common is, as UNHCR's Statute requires, that they are "devoted to the purposes of the Office of the High Commissioner".

Persons of concern to UNHCR are first of all those defined as refugees in the Statute of the Office. But the General Assembly has also called on UNHCR to assist other categories of persons. The Statute, which was written in 1950, defines a refugee falling under the mandate of UNHCR as "any person who, owing to well-founded fear of being persecuted for reasons of race, religion, nationality., or political opinion, is outside the country of his nationality and is unable or owing to such fear and for reasons other than personal convenience, is unwilling to avail himself of the protection of that country..." Since the Statute was written, however, many new and large-scale humanitarian problems around the globe have led governments to broaden the categories of persons who may be considered of concern to UNHCR.

In numerous resolutions adopted by the General Assembly since the establishment of UNHCR, the High Commissioner has been requested to assist specific groups of persons who do not necessarily fall within the definition of a refugee contained in the Statute of the Office. For instance, UNHCR has on many occasions provided emergency relief and other forms of assistance and protection to large numbers of uprooted persons whose refugee status cannot be determined individually because of the size of the group concerned, its rate of influx or the urgency of its needs. The High Commissioner has also been called upon to assist persons displaced within their own countries, as well as those who flee man-made disasters, And UNHCR has been asked to assist former refugees who have returned home as well as internally displaced persons able to return to their places of origin.

A refugee, by definition, can no longer depend on the protection of the government of his or her country of origin. UNHCR, therefore, has been entrusted with the function of providing refugees with protection, under the auspices of the United Nations. This function has come to be known as 'international protection'. First and foremost, this means that UNHCR tries to ensure that no' refugee is returned involuntarily to a country where he or she has reason to fear persecution. It also means that UNHCR promotes accessions to basic international legal instruments relating to refugees and monitors the behaviour of states to make sure that standards defined in those instruments are respected.

The most universal of these instruments is the 1951 United Nations Convention relating to the Status of Refugees, as supplemented by the 1967 United Nations Refugee Protocol, These instruments provide a definition of the term "refugee' and lay down minimum standards for the treatment of refugees. Today, 104 countries are party to one or both of these instruments. There are many other international legal instruments which are directly or indirectly concerned with refugees. One of the most important is the Convention Governing the Specific Aspects of Refugee Problems in Africa, adopted by the Organisation of African Unity in 1969.

Convention and Protocol relating to the Status of Refugees Convention

The 1951 Convention on the Status of Refugees provides the most comprehensive codification of the rights of refugees yet attempted on the international level. It lays down basic minimum standards for the treatment of refugees, without prejudice to the granting by States of more favourable treatment. The Convention provides for economic and social rights of refugees and contains various safeguards against the expulsion of refugees including the fundamental principle of non-refoulement. The Convention is to be applied without discrimination as to race, religion or country of origin. It also makes provision for the documentation of refugees, including a refugee travel document in passport form.

Protocol

The scope of the Convention is limited to persons who have become refugees as a result of events occurring before I January 1951. However, with the passage of time and the emergence of new refugee situations, the need was increasingly felt to make the provisions of the Convention applicable to such new refugees. As a result, a Protocol relating to the Status of Refugees was prepared and submitted to the United Nations General Assembly in 1966. By accession to the Protocol, States undertake to apply the substantive provisions of the 1951 Convention to all refugees covered by the definition of the latter, but without limitation of date.

Although related to the Convention in this way, the Protocol is an independent instrument, accession to which is not limited to States parties to the Convention.

UNHCR can only start material assistance programmes when it is asked by the host government to help, In many instances, the first request is for emergency relief, for such essentials as food, water, shelter and medical aid. But once the emergency phase of an operation is over, UNHCR strives to help refugees wherever possible to become self-reliant. To this end, education and vocational training programmes are set up and income-generating activities are encouraged.

There are particularly vulnerable individuals in each refugee situation. In general, UNHCR devotes special attention to unaccompanied children, disabled refugees and persons who are medically-at-risk, and the elderly. Refugee women and children are estimated to constitute over two-thirds of the world's refugee population, and special programmes are designed for them.

As soon as the immediate assistance needs of refugees have been met, the search for durable solutions begins. There are three, possible, long-term solutions: voluntary repatriation, local integration in the country of asylum, or resettlement (migration) to a second asylum country. Voluntary, repatriation is considered the preferred solution to a refugee problem, but it is not always possible, for it usually requires a fundamental change in the country of origin. UNHCR thus assists refugees to integrate in the country in which they initially sought asylum. The object of local integration is to help refugees to become self-supporting in their country of residence, and host governments are encouraged to grant them the same facilities as those to which nationals are entitled. Counselling, including legal aid to assist refugees with administrative formalities, is often needed. When local integration is not possible, UNHCR may help refugees to resettle, in other words, to find another country where they and their families are granted asylum.

UNHCR's budget varies from year to year. For 1989 UNHCR has prepared a budget for its regular, programmes of $US 419 million. In addition, the Office maintains an Emergency Fund of $US 10 million, to be able to respond to new refugee situations when ever they arise. The work of UNHCR is financed almost, entirely from voluntary contributions from Governments, non-governmental organizations and individuals. Only a very small amount is received each year from the regular budget of the United Nations and this sum may only be used to help to defray administrative costs.

In most cases, UNHCR relies on implementing partners. These partners are generally non-governmental agencies- which have long experience in refugee work and have qualified personnel with field experience. Today UNHCR is working with over 200 nongovernmental agencies to carry out its assistance programmes all over the world. But while UNHCR acts essentially as a planner and as a co-ordinator, it is ultimately responsible to the international community and to the world's refugees, for making sure that refugees receive the assistance they need.

Yes UNHCR draws on the expertise of other organizations of the United Nations system, such as the Food and Agriculture Organization (FAO), the World Health Organization (WHO), the World Food Programme (WFP) and the United Nations Development Programme (UNDP) to name only a few.

The first step to helping refugees is to understand that they are not a threat to you, but rather, they are themselves threatened. Public opinion can go a long way toward encouraging governments to adopt policies which are favourable toward refugees, both at home and abroad. For more information on what you can do in your own community, contact a voluntary agency of your choice or the UNHCR Office nearest to you.

The Responsibilities of UNHCR

The debate concerning the refugee definition is not new. Political and historical factors, more than legal ones, have led to an evolution of the term which cannot be ignored if some of the present, confusion is to be overcome. The refugee concept has its historical roots in the religious persecution of dissident groups several centimes ago. In more recent, times, this category has specifically included the victims of harsh treatment by those in power for political reasons. Early international efforts to respond to the refugee problem following the First World War focused on specific categories of persecuted minorities a Europe, who were singled out for their ethnic, political or religious origins. Persecution was the central concept in the League of Nations' efforts to respond to the victims of Nazism in this period, and was to remain the basis of the international structures set up after World War 11, primarily to assist those fleeing newly established regimes in Europe. UNHCR's Statute in 1951 similarly reflected the concept of individual or group persecution as the key element in identifying who was entitled to benefit from the new international legal structures designed to protect those who had been compelled to cross international borders.

While still relevant, this concept alone is not adequate to respond to the refugee problem today. For UNHCR, the challenge is not so much to formulate more precise legal definitions,, but to clarify the proper responsibility of the Office nearly 40 years later, although the two are of course linked. Who should UNHCR attempt to protect and assist and to what extent arc governments bound to recognize this competence ?

In lay man's terms the question is not so difficult. Starting already in the late 1950s, UNHCR was called upon by governments, through the UN, to assist, on a " good .offices " basis various categories of exiles who were not necessarily the victims of group or individual persecution. These categories soon become more numerous: displaced persons, returnees and even uprooted populations who had not left their own countries. UNHCR was asked to use its "good offices" to transmit contributions or to intervene on behalf of the Secretary-General in areas where others could not do so. In the following years, UNHCR's general humanitarian role was increasingly acknowledged by governments and by other agencies. The Office was even given some specific responsibility for stateless individuals, albeit a limited one. In Africa, this necessary change in the categories falling within UNHCR's responsibility - many of whom were fleeing the dire but general consequences of modern conflict, rather than any direct form of persecution - was formally embodied in the Organization of African Unity's Refugee Convention.

The Duty of Solidarity

The point can never be too strongly stressed: refugee movements are a contemporary scourge which spare no continent. Almost 40 years ago, the United Nations mandated my Office to find the most appropriate solutions to the problem. Through local integration and resettlement, countries of asylum have constantly helped to safeguard the unity of the family, an intangible and universally acknowledged principle. But the most natural solution is still voluntary repatriation for it enables refugees to rediscover their social and cultural roots, which give them the comforting feeling of belonging to their country of origin. It is gratifying to note that conditions in refugees' countries of origin often change to such an extent that repatriation becomes possible. In 1988 this was the case in Ethiopia, Uganda, and El Salvador, and readers of REFUGEES magazine were duly informed of these events. We enter 1989 with a renewed hope that more refugees will be granted their wish to return to their homeland. The Office of the High Commissioner, in keeping with its mandate, will naturally be there to help them.

Remarkably, 1989 will see further developments in the work carried out by the Office of the High Commissioner in over 90 countries around the world. The Executive Committee has approved a financial target for 1989 of US$ 428.7 million for which an appeal will be made to governments. It is reassuring to recall that they have never failed in their duty of solidarity towards those in need of international protection. As they peruse the pages of this special issue of REFUGEES, readers will become aware of the complexity of the task, and of the diversity of the situations that demand greater generosity from the international community as well as a desire to achieve solutions that address the refugees' most basic needs.

These adults, children and elderly people yearn for a daily life like that of "ordinary people ". I sincerely trust that the programme established by my Office - both in the field and at headquarters - will act as a foundation for the achievement of their legitimate aspirations. The letters UNHCR' stand for the Office of the United Nations High Commissioner for Refugees, a humanitarian and strictly non-political organization established by the UN General Assembly at the beginning of 1951. Based in Geneva and with more than 100 offices all around the world, UNHCR, which employs more than 2,000 persons, has two principal functions: to protect refugees and to seek permanent solutions to their plight.

Until such solutions can be found, UNHCR provides refugees with both emergency relief and longer-term assistance. In popular usage, the word "refugee" describes people in a variety of situations. But in the international context, it refers specifically to persons who are outside their country of origin and unable or unwilling to return to it, because of a well-founded fear of persecution "for reasons of race, religion, nationality, membership of a particular social group or political opinion." This definition is enshrined in the 1951 UN Convention relating to the Status of Refugees and its 1967 Protocol. These basic international instruments governing the rights and obligations of refugees have now been ratified by more than 100 different countries around the world. UNHCR's concern also extends to people who do, not fall strictly within the Convention definition: those who are compelled to leave their country because of armed conflict and civil strife; those who are in the process of submitting a claim for refugee status ("asylum seekers"); and refugees who have voluntarily decided to go back to their own country.

UNHCR is not, however, responsible for 'people who benefit from the protection or assistance of other UN organizations. The High Commissioner is elected by the UN General Assembly, on the nomination of the UN Secretary-General. The current High Commissioner, Jean-Pierre Hocke, took up his duties on 1 January 1986. The High Commissioner receives guidance from an Executive Committee, composed of 43 Member States.

One of the Executive Committee's tasks is to approve the organization's assistance programmes, and to set financial targets for their implementation. The whole of UNHCR's assistance budget is met by voluntary contributions, primarily by governments, although part of its administrative expenses are borne by the regular budget of the United Nations. UNHCR is not a permanent agency, and since 1953 its mandate has been renewed by the UN General Assembly every five years. First and foremost, UNHCR tries to ensure that no refugee is forcibly repatriated to a country where he or she would face persecution. As indicated already, UNHCR has two principal functions. First, it provides international protection to refugees, because refugees, by definition, can no longer depend on the protection of their own country. First and foremost, this means that UNHCR tries to ensure that no refugee is returned against their will to a country where he or she has reason to fear persecution. It also means that UNHCR encourages governments to sign the basic International agreements on the treatment of refugees, and monitors the behaviour of States to make sure that the standards defined in those agreements are respected. UNHCR's second important responsibility is to find durable solutions to refugee situations. There are three possible permanent solutions: voluntary repatriation to the refugee's own country; integration in the country which has granted the refugee asylum; or resettlement in a second asylum country.

Voluntary repatriation is considered the preferred solution, but is not usually possible until the circumstances which have forced a refugee to leave his or her country have ceased to exist. UNHCR, therefore, also assists refugees to integrate in their country of first asylum, helping them to become self- supporting and to be granted the same facilities as nationals. When neither of these solutions -voluntary repatriation or local integration - is possible, UNHCR may help refugees to resettle; that is to find another country where they and their families can begin a safe and productive new life. Until solutions are found for refugees', UNHCR, at the request of the host countries, provides material assistance to them. In many instances, the first request is for emergency relief, in the form of essentials such as water, food, shelter and medical aid.

But once the emergency phase is over, UNHCR strives to help refugees become self-reliant, through the introduction of education and training programmes and income-generating activities. In most cases, UNHCR relies on implementing partners - voluntary agencies, government departments and liberation movements - to implement the programmes which it finances. UNHCR also co-operates closely with other organizations of the UN system, such as the UN Development Programme, World Food Programme and World Health Organization. UNHCR devotes special attention to the particularly vulnerable people who are present in any refugee situation, most notably women, children, disabled people, the elderly and medically at risk.

International Co-operation for Refugee Protection

The UN High Commissioner for Refugees' main role is to secure international protection for refugees - a role which, with the passage of time, has developed and expanded. In this article, Ghassan Arnaout, Director of the Division of Refugee Law and Doctrine, presents the major protection problems encountered by the High Commissioner today, and underlines the need for international co-operation. There are some 12 million refugees in the world today and, in keeping with this figure, UNHCR has an annual budget of almost US$ 400 million.

These statistics say something about the magnitude of the task facing UNHCR. What they cannot describe, however, are the individual tragedies. These begin with the exile of persons from their homeland and they continue with the problems of finding a country of refuge, until a durable solution can be found.

Legal instruments cannot guarantee that refugees will be treated humanely. A practical effort is required by everyone concerned. There is a growing sense, that the "right to live in one's country" is not merely one of the many-possible solutions to the refugee problem; it is the solution. From this point of wards, any international co-operation that tackles the root causes of refugee flows, in order to stem them at source and to restore conditions conducive to voluntary repatriation, takes on a paramount importance. As protection becomes an even more complex problem in today's world, international co-operation is imperative. A formal legal regime does not itself guarantee that persons will not be exiled and that refugees will be exiled and that refugees will be treated humanely and justly. This requires a collective and concerted effort on a practical level by countries of origin, host countries, international organizations, non-governmental organizations and the refugees themselves. Multilateral consultations are the ideal meeting ground and the ideal melting pot for this sort of collective endeavour. The recent progress achieved through informal consultations on asylum in Europe, and in working group discussions on particular groups of asylum seekers, has demonstrated the value of interaction and co-operation on the practical level.

Another protection problem facing UNHCR is expulsion. Information received by UNHCR on this subject regrettably reveals that the cases recorded, far from being isolated instances, represent a growing trend, a continuing problem whose size has until now been understated. In connection with expulsion, UNHCR is confronted with the problem of push-offs of boat arrivals. When asylum seekers in boats are denied entry to a country and are obliged to continue their journey elsewhere, there is strong argument that they have, in effect, been rejected at the border. Rejection at the frontier is increasingly recognized as constituting refoulement, as it leads to expelling or returning a refugee to the frontiers of a country where that person's life or freedom are threatened.

In some countries, the conditions of detention for refugees and asylum seekers defy all standards of basic decency and common humanity. Detention without justifiable' cause has increased. The detention of asylum seekers and refugees also continues to be a matter of serious concern. UNHCR field offices throughout the world report that detention conditions in some countries defy all standards of basic decency and common humanity. Detention without justifiable cause, often under harsh conditions, has increased, in total disregard of the minimum restraints recognized as applicable under such circumstances by the UNHCR Executive Committee. Furthermore, the security of refugees continues to be threatened in a number of countries. There are repeated military attacks on refugee camps and settlements, in defiance of international law. Deplorably, not a month passes without UNHCR being informed of attacks on areas where large numbers of refugees are concentrated, in which there is loss of civilian life and untold suffering.

Whether these attacks are carried out by state armies in an effort to harass refugees and undermine the institution of asylum, or by groups of insurgents in search of supplies and forcibly recruiting refugees, they must be condemned by the entire international community as an unacceptable practice. To ensure prompt action, UNHCR must be informed more rapidly and fully about such attacks, and it must also have authorized access to the affected areas. The Office is working to increase its capacity, and together with the United Nations Secretary-General, attempting to coordinate more closely within the UN system to deal with this tragic problem.

The forced conscription of refugees for short or longer periods, into the, regular or irregular armed forces of parties to a conflict, is another and particularly complex protection problem. Not only does this practice seriously endanger the lives of those directly involved, and of their families, it can also jeopardize their refugee status and compromise the humanitarian and civilian character of the camps in which they live. Unfortunately, this is a continuing practice which will require further considerable efforts. This year, for the first time, the attention of the Executive Committee was drawn to an issue in the area of social and economic rights. Appreciation of the close linkage between the welfare of nationals and successful self-sufficiency programmes for refugees has led UNHCR to implement projects of benefit to both nationals and refugees, and in a broader sense, to the host country. These programmes are designed to make it easier for refugees to find work. Gainful employment is a vital element of self-sufficiency, and is essential to the process of realizing durable solutions to refugee problems. UNHCR encourages all States hosting refugees to examine their own laws and practices with a view to identifying existing obstacles to refugee employment and, where necessary, to take steps to remove these obstacles. One vexing issue which complicates discussions with governments is the question of international responsibility towards asylum seekers.

It is perhaps useful to remember that a refugee becomes a refugee not by virtue of being formally determined as such - this merely certifies the fact - but at a much earlier point in time, when he or she is forced to flee his or her country because of prevailing circumstances: Hence, many asylum seekers are refugees even in the absence of any formal determination of their status.

The prospects for increased international understanding are now bright. The return of thousands of exiles to their homelands would be a most rewarding outcome of United Nations peace efforts. There are certain rights, such as the right not to be 'refouled', which, because of their fundamental nature, do not depend on formal recognition of status. The Executive Committee took a similar position in 1981 in Conclusion 22. This Conclusion acquires full significance in the present context in that it reflects a significant measure of

State agreement on responsibilities towards asylum seekers, regardless of any ruling on the question of refugee status. The Executive Committee has, on a number of occasions, endorsed the idea that asylum seekers attract international responsibility. Obviously not all asylum seekers will remain the concern of the High Commissioner, nor attract the whole range of responsibilities on the part of States.

But the substance of responsibility towards asylum seekers undoubtedly requires more precise definition. With the aim not only of averting new influxes of refugees but also to enable durable solutions to be found for existing situations, it is of cardinal importance to come to grips with the root causes of refugee flows. Some of these situations have existed for a number of years and efforts to find a solution have foundered on the inability, or the unwillingness of States to work together in a spirit of international solidarity to resolve political differences and to restore international peace. Hence the need for international co-operation in a multilateral context. The main humanitarian problems of our time, of which refugees are one facet, have an international dimension both in their nature and their source.

Multilateral diplomacy, in which the UN and its bodies take on the role of catalyst, has in the past come under strong criticism for its failure to provide viable solutions to particularly obdurate problems. There is a surge of renewed interest in the UN as a focal point for international solidarity and co-operation. What we have witnessed, over the last year, has been an awareness by States of the need for multilateral diplomacy in settling international disputes. A new dynamism is now afoot in the arena of international affairs, which has enabled the UN to come into its own once again as a peacebroker and an enforcer of human rights. The United Nations can be as successful as its member states allow it to be. It is perhaps no exaggeration to say that the prospects for international peace and mutual understanding have never been brighter since the end of World War II. The Cold War has given way to a greater respect for the principles of co-existence and co-operation. If prospects for peace can be advanced to their logical conclusion, refugees will be among the first to benefit. The return of hundreds of thousands of exiles would indeed be the most rewarding outcome of the United Nations' efforts, including those to resolve the Afghan crisis, the Gulf War, the Sahrawi problem in the Maghreb, conflicts in Namibia and Angola, the ethnic crisis in Sri Lanka, the adversities in Cambodia and the problems of the Horn of Africa.

As part of the United Nations, UNHCR is, of course, happy to play its part in contributing to these multilateral efforts. The accession of more States to the international refugee instruments and their active co-operation with UNHCR, will make our role more universal and will also make our task of finding solutions to refugee problems very much easier.

The 1989 UNHCR budgetary allocations for Europe and North-America, approved by the Executive Committee, total US$ 19,9 million. This amount represents the contribution of the international community to assistance and services provided to refugees and asylum seekers by and through non-governmental organizations in various countries and complements the support available to refugees from government programmes. Specifically it covers activities in the field of legal and social counselling to asylum seekers; assistance to aged, handicapped and otherwise vulnerable refugees; and finally, care and maintenance for refugees and asylum seekers in need in those countries where no other sources of support are available.

Governments are alarmed by the arrival of asylum seekers. Many have taken steps to exclude them by introducing a variety of restrictive and deterrent measures. The number of asylum applications in Europe has steadily increased since the second halt of the 1980s, virtually doubling from some 104,000 in 1984 to more than 180,000 in 1987. Latest estimates suggest that the number of new applications in 1988 may have exceeded 200,000. However, these figures are open to query. Different registration criteria and statistical methods as well as the movement of some asylum seekers from one country to another undoubtedly lead to double counting, so that the actual figures are, in all probability, lower than those reported by governments.

Freedom of Movement

Nonetheless, these numbers of arrivals, the fact that some two-thirds of all asylum seekers in recent years came from outside Europe, and the prospect that by 1992 freedom of movement of persons throughout the European Community may become a reality, have caused considerable concern to governments. Many have responded by introducing measures designed to discourage requests and restrict entry possibilities. These measures range from narrowing interpretations of the refugee definition, the introduction of new visa requirements and criteria for asylum applications, to sanctions against transport companies. Their vigorous application has raised the risk of refoulement of asylum seekers and refugees, and increased the number of cases of persons stranded at borders and airports. Additionally, the fate of persons in need of international protection because their lives, security and liberty are at risk in their home countries, but who do not strictly fulfil the criteria of the 1951 UN Convention and the 1967 Protocol relating to the Status of, Refugees, has been placed in jeopardy.

A global approach to the problem is needed to prevent the abuse of asylum procedures and to maintain proper safeguards for the protection of refugees and asylum seekers. Similarly restrictive measures prevail in North America, with the introduction of new legislation on immigration in the United States and in Canada. Although refugee admission quotas have remained high in the United States and considerable efforts are being undertaken in Canada to deal with the existing backlog in refugee status determination procedures, it remains to be seen how the new legislation will affect first asylum cases as well as the numbers of resettlement opportunities open to asylum seekers in both countries. UNHCR will maintain and intensify its consultations with all the governments concerned, convinced that a global approach to the problem is required to prevent the abuse of asylum procedures and maintain proper safeguard for the protection of refugees and asylum seekers. In Europe, where government efforts at harmonizing policies, procedures and criteria have moved apace at regional level, UNHCR will continue to be available to assist in efforts to formulate common guidelines for the treatment of asylum applications. Although considerable difficulties arise from the varied legal procedures and traditions and the special conditions prevailing in eastern and southern Europe, consultations between governments have been marked by a generally forward looking and concerned approach. "Have refugees become the new 'untouchables' of the late 20th century ? " the High Commissioner asked some time ago. It is to be hoped that, efforts of UNHCR, strongly supported by many non-governmental organizations and a concerned and informed public, notwithstanding the prevailing unfavourable economic climate and rising poverty in 'rich' countries, will arrest the trend of rejecting asylum seekers and avoid the erosion of the concept of asylum.

For industrialized countries without accurate refugee population data, UNHCR has estimated the refugee population based on recent refugee arrivals and recognition as well as estimates for temporary protection. The statistics presented here do not cover Palestinian refugees who come under the mandate of the United Nations Relief and Works Agency for Palestinian Refugees in the Near East (UNRWA). For the purpose of these statistics, the 1998 -total population of concern to UNHCR has been defined as follows:

- Refugees: persons recognized as refugees under the 1951 United Nations Convention relating to the Status of Refugees or its 1967 Protocol, the 1969 Organization of African Unity (OAU) Convention Governing the Specific Aspects of Refugee Problems in Africa, persons recognized as refugees in accordance with the UNHCR Statute, persons granted humanitarian status and those granted temporary protection.
- Returned refugees or "returnees": refugees who have repatriated voluntarily to their place of origin and who remain of concern to UNHCR for a limited period after their return. For the purpose of these statistics, a cut-off period of two years has been applied.
- Asylum-seekers: persons whose applications for asylum are pending in the asylum procedure or who are otherwise registered as asylum-seekers.
- Certain specific groups of persons not coming within the ordinary mandate of UNHCR, but to whom the Office extends protection and/ or assistance pursuant to a special request by a competent organ of the United Nations. This category comprises certain groups of internally displaced, including re turned

internally displaced, certain groups of war victims, certain nationals of the former Soviet Union whose nationality is undetermined and who have not established a national bond with any of the, countries which emerged following the dissolution of the Soviet Union, etc.

In recent years, UNHCR's involvement with persons who have not crossed an international border, such as the internally displaced, refugees who have returned home ("returnees") and persons threatened with displacement by, or otherwise at risk from armed conflict, has increased substantially. In view of the above, and taking into consideration the rise in the number of persons granted temporary protection and those allowed to remain in countries of asylum on humanitarian grounds, the term "refugee" needs to be qualified by an indication of the group concerned. In this report, terms "'refugees and others of concern to UNHCR", "total population of concern to UNHCR", etc. have been used to reflect these various categories.

While efforts have been made to make these statistics as comprehensive as possible, it should be noted that there are populations and movements that are not known to UNHCR because, inter alia, the Office is not directly involved, government records are lacking, etc. For instance, whereas in developing countries repatriation is difficult to verify because most refugees return by their own means, industrialized countries generally lack a refugee register through which increases and, in particular, decreases in the refugee population can be traced..

UNHCR Assistance

There is a strong correlation between UNHCR's population statistics and its assistance programmes. Indeed, one of the major reasons for the Office to collect, compile and report statistics is to indicate the size and major characteristics of populations who benefit from assistance programmes. Often, the assistance is provided through governmental, intergovernmental or non-governmental "implementing partners". Assistance is provided to those who cannot meet their own basic needs, and in the absence of other resources. UNHCR distinguishes five types of assistance:

- *emergency assistance,* which includes measures to meet basic needs, usually in case of a new refugee influx. The assistance does not normally exceed a period of twelve months,
- *care and maintenance,* which covers assistance once survival is no longer threatened. It involves meeting basic needs on a more routine basis, pending the identification of durable solutions (that is, voluntary repatriation, local settlement and resettlement). Assistance usually takes the form of providing food, water, household utensils, medical care, shelter, transportation, basic education, vocational training, etc.;
- *voluntary repatriation,* which covers preparations for departure to the country of origin, transportation, etc. In most cases, it also involves activities in the country of origin, including organizing reception facilities and assistance during the initial phase of reintegration;
- *local settlement assistance,* which may be provided to refugees who cannot return home. It alms to promote their self-sufficiency and local integration;
- *resettlement,* which may be offered to refugees who are admitted temporarily to a country of asylum, who cannot return to their home country and who

face particular protection problems. UNHCR facilitates permanent settlement in third countries through securing resettlement places, medical screening, arranging for travel and measures to facilitate the integration of the refugee in the country of resettlement.

In this report, the term "UNHCR-assisted" is used to reflect the beneficiaries of these various assistance activities.

Some Practical Problems in Counting Refugees

In addition to the factors mentioned above, counting refugees poses a challenge in the following situations:

- in emergency situations, it is often not possible to provide a reliable estimate, owing to the ongoing nature of the influx;
- in large-scale refugee situations, camp populations are often "fluid", that is they move in and out of camps, often without notifying UNHCR or the local authorities. "Closed" camps, where the movement of residents is subject to control, are an exception;
- only a few of the industrialized countries maintain a refugee register recording the increases and decreases in the refugee population. Thus, the available information is usually limited to the inflow of refugees and asylum-seekers and to individual refugee status determination. Information on decreases in the refugee population, including naturalization, spontaneous departures, emigration and cessation of refugee status, is usually not available;
- as increases in the refugee population are better recorded than decreases, there is a tendency, both in more developed countries and in countries where

refugees are assisted by UNHCR, to over-estimate refugee numbers;

- statistics can become quickly outdated as a result of sudden new arrivals or departures;
- significant forced displacements may go un- or underreported. Thus, in a number of instances, UNHCR is unable to establish or verify the total refugee population in the country, but can only collect information on those refugees with whom the Office has come into contact.

Total Population of Concern to UNHCR

From the end of 1997 to the end of 1998, the total indicative total population of concern to UNHCR fell from 22.4 million to 21.5 million, a decrease of some 4 per cent. Whereas Africa-experienced a-significant-decline (-15 per cent), the total population of concern in other regions remained fairly stable. *The global refugee population* estimated by UNHCR also fell by some 4 per cent during 1398. The largest decline was recorded in Latin America and the Caribbean (-11 per cent), followed by Europe (-9 per cent) and Africa (-6 per cent). The estimated *asylum-seeker population* rose by some 38 per cent during 1998. This increase is mainly the result of significantly higher estimate for Germany; whereas the 1997 asylum seeker estimate for Germany (34,900) was based on the number of pending cases in first instance, the current estimate (370,000) reflects the number of asylum-seekers whose applications are pending in all instances.

During 1998, some 986,000 refugees repatriated voluntarily, seven per cent more than during 1997 (921,000). The returnee population of concern to UNHCR, defined as those refugees who returned during 1997 and 1998, reached 1.9 million persons by the end of 1998, a decline of 38 per

PERSONS OF CONCERN TO UNHCR

As of 1 January 2007, UNHCR reported a total of 21 018 589 individuals falling under its mandate.

- 7979251 in Asia, of which
- 2580638 in the Middle-East
- 2974315 in South-East Asia
- 218584 in Central Asia
- 1304189 in South Asia
- 901525 in East Asia and the Pacific
- 4740392 in Europe, of which
- 1617214 in Eastern Europe
- 708132 in South-East Europe
- 616132 in Central Europe and in the Baltic states
- 1798914 in Western Europe
- 5069123 in Africa, of which
- 1359175 in Central Africa and the Great Lakes region
- 2105314 in Eastern Africa
- 1031030 in Western Africa
- 434427 in the Southern African region
- 139177 in North Africa
- 3229822 in America, of which
- 717545 in North America and in the Caribbean
- 2512277 in South America

cent compared to the returnee population of concern to UNHCR at the end of 1997 (3,055,000). The indicative number of others of concern to UNHCR increased from 6,3 9 1, 900 at the end of 1997 to 6,741,500 at the end of 1998, a rise of almost 6 per cent. This increase was largely caused by a change in the estimate for internally displaced persons in Sri Lanka, from 200,000 in 1997 to 600,000 in 1998. By the end of 1998, Asia hosted the largest number of refugees (41 per cent), followed by Africa (28 per cent), Europe (23 per cent), North America (6 per cent), Latin America and the Caribbean and Oceania (each I per cent). Asia hosts 35 per cent of the total population of concern to UNHCR, Africa and Europe host each 29 per cent, whereas North America accounts for 6 per cent. Latin America and the Caribbean and Oceania each host less than one per cent of the total population of concern to UNHCR.

Staffing

The UNHCR employs a staff of approximately 6,300 people in more than 110 countries.

High Commissioners

The post of High Commissioner has been held by:

- António Guterres, 2005–present (term extended another 5 years in 2010) (Portugal)
- Ruud Lubbers, 2001–2005 (the Netherlands)
- Sadako Ogata, 1990–2000 (Japan)
- Thorvald Stoltenberg, January–November 1990 (Norway)
- Jean-Pierre Hocké, 1986–1989 (Switzerland)
- Poul Hartling, 1978–1985 (Denmark)
- Prince Sadruddin Aga Khan, 1965–1977 (Iran)

- Félix Schnyder, 1960–1965 (Switzerland)
- Auguste R. Lindt, 1956–1960 (Switzerland)
- Gerrit Jan van Heuven Goedhart, 1951–1956 (the Netherlands)

Prior to the establishment of UNHCR, Fridtjof Nansen was the League of Nations High Commissioner of the International Office for Refugees, from 1922.

Goodwill Ambassadors

UNHCR is also represented by a number of UNHCR Goodwill Ambassadors, who at present are Barbara Hendricks, Adel Imam, Angelina Jolie, Giorgio Armani, Boris Trajanov, Julien Clerc, George Dalaras, Osvaldo Laport, Khaled Hosseini and Muazzez Ersoy. Previous ambassadors include Richard Burton, Nazia Hassan, James Mason and Sophia Loren.

By the end of 1998, Afghans were the largest refugee population, numbering some 2.6 million persons. It should be noted, however, that information on the origin of refugee population is not available for a number of countries, particularly those in Europe and North America [For latest figures of refugee population in the world see Box in pages 2-7 of this book.]

4

Refugees in SAARC Region

> "Bodily exercises, when compulsory, do no harm to the body; but knowledge which is acquired under compulsion obtains no hold on the mind."
>
> —*Plato*

It is pertinent to note thate more than 1.2 billion or over one fifth of humanity live in the countries of the SAARC region. According to the current population trends in the region, India will overtake China as the most populated country in the world and Pakistan will be more populated than either USA or Russia in the coming decades. Bangladesh and Nepal population are projected to grow at the rate of 2.5 percent a year. Hence, movements of populations across borders whether they are economic migrants or political refugees will continue to engage the policy makers as a key component of the regional humanitarian agenda. From a population displacement perspective, South Asia region has a unique history. The States of India and Pakistan and later Bangladesh got defined from massive refugee movements. After 1947 partition 7.5 million Hindu and Sikh refugees from Pakistan crossed over to India and 7.2 million Muslim refugees from India crossed to Pakistan. It was the largest recorded refugee movement in history. There was no or little international assistance in this massive and painful humanitarian crisis. In 1979,10 million Bengalis crossed to India during the war of independence of Bangladesh. In 1979. 3.5 million Afghans fleeing Soviet intervention in that country sought and received asylum in Pakistan of which 1.2 million are still languishing in the refugee villages. In 1992, Bangladesh was inundated for a second time in recent history with the influx of 250,000 Muslim refugees from Rakhine district in Myanmar of whom nearly 30,000 refugees had still failed to repatriate. Similarly, 90,000 Bhutanese of Nepali origin were expelled and are still located in refugee camps in Jhapa district of Nepal.

Sri Lanka, despite her insular position was once described in a USCR report as an "Island of Refugees" due to external displacement of Tamils and internal displacements of Sinhalese, Tamil and Muslims. Sri Lanka never known as an asylum country but is well known as a refugee producing country. Since 1983, Sri Lanka, has produced apart from over 500,000 Sri Lankan Tamil "jet refugees" to the western world; three waves of Tamil refugees to India in 1983-87; 1990-91 and after April 1995. Major portion of Sri Lankan refugees in Tamil Nadu had voluntarily repatriated but still some 60,000 have remained behind due to the ongoing security crisis in North-East Sri Lanka. Since 1960's, India hosts over 100,000 Tibetan refugees and some 50,000 Buddhist Chakma refugees from Chittagong hill tracts in Bangladesh-some of whom repatriated recently under a political settlement. India also has permitted UNHCR to assist 20.000 Afghan refugees on pure humanitarian grounds. Maldives is the only SAARC country who neither produced nor hosted a significant refugee population.

Despite these past and existing refugee movements and deep rooted humanitarian traditions of asylum, none of the SAARC countries have acceded to the 1951 International

Convention on Refugees or its 1967 Protocol which had been ratified by 136 countries in the world. However, all the SAARC countries other than Bhutan and Maldives have offices of the United Nations High Commissioner for Refugees, (UNHCR) the UN agency responsible for the promotion of the Refugee Instruments and marshaling of international humanitarian assistance on behalf of the refugees. UNHCR provides international protection and assistance to Afghan and Iraqi refugees in Pakistan. In India, UNHCR provides assistance to some 20,000 urban Afghan refugees and from Madras, monitors the voluntary nature of the Sri Lankan Tamil refugee repatriation.

UNHCR also provides assistance to the government of Nepal to look after the asylum seekers from Bhutan and monitors the repatriation of Rohinghya refugees from Bangladesh to Myanmar. In view of the importance of UNHCR's role in refugee matters, Bangladesh, India and Pakistan applied and became members of UNHCR's Executive Committee, the highest policy making body in the Organization. They have played an active role in the deliberations of refugee policy during the past few years. The gamut of reasons adduced for the non accession to the 1951 Convention of the 1967 Protocol by SAARC countries other than the island states are very similar in content. They argue that they have rich traditions of asylum comparable with international standards some times even going beyond what was practiced by some of the party signatories to the International Refugee Instruments.

Therefore, they would continue to deal with refugee issues on an ad hoc bi-lateral policy basis but welcomed international humanitarian assistance on the basis of burden sharing. (India is an exception). SAARC countries further argue that the persecution based 1951 Convention or 1967 refugee issues in the region which were mostly the result of internal conflicts and not due to fear of persecution by the states per se. In support of their contention that the International Refugee Instruments were inadequate, they cite the regional refugee instruments of Africa, the 1958 Organization of African Unity (OAU) Convention and on refugees in Latin America, the 1984 Cartagena Declaration on refugees. It is in the above context, that a regional convention or a declaration on refugees by the SAARC countries becomes timely and relevant.

SAARC Charter provides against discussion of bilateral and contentious issues. Summit retreats had somewhat overcome this limitation. Refugee issues when discussed bilaterally without regional or international commitment to a set of guiding principles, could become contentious. Refugee situations in South Asia had become chronic and has affected both national security and inter-state relations due to the reluctance of states to discuss them on pure humanitarian basis. A regional agreement of fundamental questions such as the definition of a refugee, the granting of asylum and the exceptions thereto, the cardinal principle of non-refoulement, or the voluntary nature of eventual repatriation of refugees would reduce the room for friction between the state interlocutors. A SAARC Refugee, Convention/Declaration would also mean a great step forward in developing a humanitarian law regime in the region.

The immediate beneficiaries would of course be the refugees themselves in different SAARC countries of whom over 70% are women and children. In the absence of a normative refugee standards, refugees in South Asia, today, live in fear of capricious actions by refugee officials. Since all refugees are technically considered illegal aliens, they have no institutional protection or the protection of the principle of the Rule of Law. In the case of India, the Superior Courts had addressed certain humanitarian concerns of Refugees on the basis of constitutionally guaranteed fundamental and human rights. (See national Human Rights Commission Vs Union of India 1996(1) sec 295). But no such developments had taken place in any other SAARC countries. The prevailing political and security preoccupation's of each country determines the standards of treatment of refugees.

These standards may differ from time to time, from one country to another or the whims and fancies of the refugee officials. In short, article 14 of the Universal Declaration of Human Rights:- 'Everyone has the fight to seek and enjoy asylum from persecution's reduced to hollow international legal rhetoric. In developing a regional convention/declaration on refugees, SAARC countries would only be recognizing and refining the existing traditional humanitarian policies. They will be developing a set of non-contentious humanitarian principles which will enhance the organizational solidarity and its commitment to respect human rights. It will further strengthen SAARC position in the international fora, such a convention or declaration would not be a document borrowed from outside not suitable for specific needs of the problem of refugees in the region but a SAARC developed piece of international law. 1987 SAARC Regional Convention on the Suppression of Terrorism was ten years ahead of the United Nations in passing a similar convention.

SAARC Convention on Suppression of Terrorism dealt with politically more sensitive and contentious subject and there were grave doubts whether a regional consensus could be reached. But displaying the commitment of SAARC Countries in finding solutions to common regional problems, the agreement was reached well before anticipated. In addition to terrorism, SAARC agreements had been reached on non-political subjects such as trade and tourism contributing to the development of a regional legal regime in South Asia.

However, certain institutional and political constraints prevented SAARC Countries taking any measures towards adoption of a Regional approach to the question of refugees. Institutionally, SAARC is yet to develop the capacity to innovate regional approaches to international law questions. The provision in SAARC Charter to avoid contentious issues have inhibited initiatives except in technical and economical fields. Even though the main non governmental SAARC sub - group the SAARC LAW comprising of judges, legal academics and lawyers from the SAARC member countries have shown interest in developing regional instruments, absence of an institutional process to advance such ideas have stalled the discussions. Refugee issues is yet, to enter the main domestic political debate in the SAARC countries. Refugee policy had been left to the bureaucratic decision makers who typically prefers to maintain status quo where they retain authority on the subject.

Another reason that prevent-political leadership in South Asia discussing the issue of refugees at regional level is related to the leverage that certain countries receive by hosting refugees. Grant of asylum and facilitating repatriation are seen as political acts rather than humanitarian. The decisions in respect to refugees if limited by International or Regional norms would affect the, manoeuvrability of the policy makers. Unlike the case of Human Rights or issues of women and children there had been no international interest in promoting awareness on refugee questions in South Asia. In fact many of the refugees hosted by the developed countries in the world had their origins in South Asia. The Afghans, Sikhs and Sri Lankan Tamils are among the leading groups that pressurized the asylum systems in Europe, North America and Australia. These developed countries had gradually developed stricter asylum policies in their countries and can not be expected to promote refugee concepts in South Asia. Finally, in view of multicultural composition of South Asian Society the political leadership considers it prudent to de-emphasize divisive refugee issues: Disruption of ethnic homogeneity which had resulted from many refugee flows in the region is a phenomenon to he discouraged and to be shelved.

Steps towards a Regional Instrument

Some preliminary steps helpful to develop a regional convention/declaration on refugees have already been taken both at the governmental and non-governmental level. As far back as 1966, inter governmental Asian Afriçan Legal Consultative Committee (AALCC) in its meeting in Bangkok after much discussion declared a set of "Principles concerning the Treatment of Refugees" Even though, the principles, were of guiding nature, the participation of the governmental delegations from India, Pakistan and *Sri* Lanka in the process is of legal significance for a similar SAARC endeavor in the future. Subsequent AALCC meetings held in 1970 in Accra, and 1987 in Bangkok have added addenda to the Bangkok Principles. Again, the above mentioned intergovernmental Asian-African Legal Consultative Committee, meeting in New Delhi in 1991, commended the ratification of the 1951 Convention or its 1967 Protocol to its member states and went on to direct the AALCC secretariat to prepare a model refugee legislation that will facilitate refugee related legislation in member countries which included countries in Asia, Africa and the Middle East. In the context of SAARC, a non-governmental seminar was organized by SAARC LAW in New Delhi in May 1996 to discus the issue of refugees. The

Participants mostly legal and judicial personalities were of the view that a discussion on a regional declaration should be proceeded by the development of a model national legislation. Initiatives at the governmental level were supplemented by the present Informal Consultations on Refugees and Migratory flows in South Asia, where eminent personalities of the South Asian countries discuss the problems of refugees and solutions in an informal set up.

The Indian group is led by Justice P.N. Bhagwati, the former Chief Justice, the Bangladesh group by Dr. Kamal Hossein, the Former Foreign Minister. Pakistan group was led by late Justice Dorab Patel and now Justice Nasim Hassan Shah, former Chief Justice and the Nepal group by Mr. Risikesh Shah a Former Foreign Minister and now by Justice Vishwabath Upadhayaya, former Chief Justice and Mr. Y.K. Silwal a former SAARC Secretary General. Sri Lankan group is led by Mr. Bradman Weerakoon the Former Presidential Advisor on Foreign Affairs. The Eminent Persons Groups (EPG) met in Geneva (1994), Colombo (1995), New Delhi (1996) and Dhaka (1997) and in Kathmandu in 1998. Consensus was reached in the EPG consultations on the crucial definition of a refugee more appropriate to the South Asian situation. In the Colombo meeting in 1995, the EPG decided to commend a definition of a refugee which was wider in scope than the 1951 definition and more in line with the broad definition contained in the Latin American Cartagena Declaration on Refugees (1984).

The informal Consultations had included in its definition of a refugee not only the fundamental elements contained in the refugee definitions in 1951 Convention, 1966 Bangkok Principles, and 1969 OAU Definition but following the 1984 Cartagena Declaration included "serious disturbance of public order, external aggression or serious violation of human rights" as additional grounds under which one could seek determination as a refugee. The Model Law categorically excludes those persons who commit crimes against peace war crimes or crimes against humanity or non-political crimes from refugee status. In the 1996 session of Informal Consultations held in New Delhi, it was decided in the context of a discussion on a draft regional declaration on refugees presented by the EPG group from Pakistan, that a EPG sub group should be established to pre pare a Model National Law chaired by Justice P.N. Bhagwati.

The draft Model Law included the broader definition of a refugee agreed at the Colombo session and incorporated number of new features hitherto not found in any of the international or regional refugee instruments. After extensive discussions, the Model Law was approved at 1997 Dhaka sessions of the Informal Consultations. Dhaka sessions also requested the respective country EPG groups to share the Model Law with their Governments so as to generate a discussion on the need for SAARC countries to develop a Regional Convention/Declaration and promote a basis for national legislation on Refugees. The Model National Law on refugees is a modern comprehensive piece of legislation. The Model Law contains elements not found in existing refugee instruments such as requirement to give special consideration to their protection and material well-being in the case of refugee women and children".

The Model Law establishes not only the rights of the refugees but also include their duties and provide for group determination of refugee status in the context of the modem phenomenon of mass refugee exodus where individual determination is impractical. The, provision regarding the cardinal principle of non-refoulment include not only refugees but also the asylum seekers where as the most appropriate solution to the problem of refugees, the principle of voluntary repatriation had been- fully refined in the Model Law.

Follow up Strategy

Informal consultations serves a useful purpose of keeping refugee issues in the forefront of the regional humanitarian agenda. This had not happened in South Asia before, Despite the informal nature of the consultations there had been interaction and dialogue between government and judicial leaders during the previous meetings. Even though consultations had not yielded any tangible results in the form of governmental legislative actions or SAARC initiatives the process need to be continued at least until all the countries in the SAARC have become the venue of the meetings at least once.

The National Model Law approved in the 1997 Dhaka sessions could be considered a singular achievement of the consultations. During the past year Eminent Persons Groups in individual countries have informally brought the attention of concerned authorities to the National Model Law. In the absence of any immediate political dividends for flagging the issue the political leadership had maintained its usual disinterest. There is a need to bring the National Model Law formally to the attention of the SAARC governments. This could originate from the office of UNHCR. Kathmandu meeting of the informal consultations could resolve to forward National Model Law to the High Commissioner for her consideration with a request to bring the same to the attention of the countries in the SAARC region. Such a request is likely to evoke a response. Another significant step that could be taken to develop a SAARC interest on refugee issues is to promote a cooperation agreement between SAARC Secretariat and UNHCR.

Agreements of cooperation already exists between SAARC Secretariat and other UN agencies. Few years ago the initial steps were taken to initiate a dialogue leading to a cooperation agreement. Informal consultations could recommend to UNHCR to pursue the matter as cooperation with SAARC would be essential for the promotion of refugee law on regional basis.

5

Major Human Rights Instruments

"No grand idea was ever born in a conference, but a lot of foolish ideas have died there."

—F. Scott Fitzgerall

The Universal Declaration of Human Rights

The task of setting out the rights and freedoms proclaimed in the Charter began as soon as the UN was created. In 1948 the Universal Declaration of Human Rights was proclaimed through a resolution passed by the General Assembly. The Universal Declaration was established "as a common standard of achievement for all peoples and all nations". It sets out in 30 articles the human rights and fundamental freedoms which the UN's Member States must respect and whose "universal recognition and observance" they are to secure.

Rights proclaimed in the Universal Declaration of Human Rights include:

- right to life, liberty and security of the person; freedom from slavery or servitude;
- freedom from torture or cruel, inhuman or degrading treatment;
- recognition as a person before the law,
- equality before the law and equal protection of the

law; freedom from arbitrary arrest, detention or exile right to a fair trial; freedom from arbitrary interference with privacy, family, home or correspondence; freedom of movement and residence within' a country;

- right to leave one's country and to return;
- right to seek asylum;
- right to a nationality;
- right to marry and found a family;
- equality of men and women in marriage and in its dissolution;
- right to own property and not be arbitrarily deprived of it;
- freedom of religion, opinion, expression and association;
- right to take part in government and equal access to public service;
- right to social security;
- right to work and to free choice of employment;
- right to rest and leisure;
- right to education;
- right to an adequate standard of living.

The Universal Declaration is not a treaty. As a resolution of the General Assembly it is not open to UN Member States to sign it or to agree to become legally bound to its provisions as such. When the Universal Declaration was being drafted it was agreed that its provisions would be further elaborated in treaties which would create binding legal obligations for state's party to them. However, the fact that the Universal Declaration is not a treaty does not diminish its importance:

- its purpose was to provide an authoritative understanding: of the human rights guaranteed in the UN Charter;
- it is the most well known UN catalogue of human rights, and it includes civil and political, as well as economic, social and cultural rights; and
- its importance has been consistently reaffirmed in resolutions of the General Assembly, and many national constitutions make reference to it or incorporate its provisions.

The International Bill of Human Rights

The codification of international customary law in the Universal Declaration into binding treaties is an ongoing process. In 1966,

- the International Covenant on Economic, Social and Cultural Rights, and
- the International Covenant on Civil and Political Rights

were adopted and transformed an important set of human rights into binding conventional instruments. Both the International Covenant on Economic, Social and Cultural Rights, and the International Covenant on Civil and Political Rights have been ratified by over 125 states. The two covenants together with the Universal Declaration are known as the International Bill of Human Rights.

Other Human Rights Treaties

The international Covenants are the most important human rights treaties as they are global and cover the main universally agreed human rights and fundamental freedoms. However, the evolution of standard -setting in human rights which began with the Universal Declaration did not end with the covenants. There are a number of other international treaties, some of them quite recent, which deal with specific rights or freedoms, or address the situation of particular groups, or seek to prevent discrimination in more detail than do the covenants. They include:

Conventions Dealing with Specific Human Rights

- Convention on the Prevention and Punishment of the Crime of Genocide (1948)
- Convention against Torture and Other Cruel, Inhuman or Degrading Treatment or Punishment (1984)

Conventions Dealing with Particular Groups

The four Geneva Conventions providing, inter alia, standards of humane treatment for prisoners and civilians in time of armed conflict (1949) and the two Additional Protocols relating to the protection of victims of international and non-international armed conflict (1977)

- Convention relating to the Status of Refugees (1951) and Protocol (1967)
- Convention relating to the Status of Stateless Persons (1954)
- Convention on the Reduction of Statelessness (1961)
- Convention on the Rights of the Child (1989)
- International Convention on the Protection of the Rights of All Migrant Workers and Members, of Their Families (1990, not yet in force)

Conventions Dealing with Discrimination

- International Convention on the Elimination of All Forms of Racial Discrimination (1965)

- Convention on the Elimination of All Forms of Discrimination against Women (1979)

It is important that UNHCR protection officers are aware of the status regarding the ratification of the various international human rights instruments by the country they are working in. The Centre for Human Rights issues every 6 months a consolidated Status of Ratification to international human rights instruments (ST/HR/4).

The information can be had from the official website also. When you want to know whether a state is party to a certain international instrument and/or how many states are party to that instrument, in the REFWORLD databases enter the Legal Databases: under this heading you will find REFINT. When you have found the appropriate instrument there will be a box for state parties, which includes numbers of ratifications, signatures and the names of state parties. Check, for example, how many states now have ratified the International Covenant on Civil and Political Rights, as well as which countries in the region you are presently working in have done so.

Other Relevant Instruments

Besides these and other treaties dealing with human rights, there are many declarations, resolutions or other decisions of UN bodies which set out human rights standards. Declarations in particular are a step in the evolution of international standard setting. They can often lead the way to ward a later treaty, as the Universal Declaration did for the International Covenants, and in any event express the political, if not yet legal, consensus of the international community on addressing a certain problem. Some of these instruments most relevant to the work of UNHCR are as follows:

Standards Dealing with Specific Human Rights

- Declaration on Territorial Asylum (1967)
- Principles on the Effective Prevention and Investigation of Extra-legal, Arbitrary and Summary Executions (1989)
- Declaration on the Protection of All Persons from Enforced Disappearance (1992)

Standards Dealing with Particular Groups

- Standard Minimum Rules for the Treatment of Prisoners (1955)
- Body of Principles for the Protection of All Persons under Any Form of Detention or Imprisonment (1988)
- United Nations Rules for the Protection of Juveniles Deprived of their Liberty (1990)
- Declaration on the Rights of Disabled Persons (1975)
- Declaration on the Rights of Persons Belonging to National or Ethnic, Religious and Linguistic Minorities (19192)
- Declaration on the Elimination of Violence against Women (1993)

Standards Dealing with Discrimination

- Declaration on the Elimination of All Forms of Intolerance, and of Discrimination Based on Religion or Belief (1981)

UN Bodies Dealing with Human Rights

The main UN bodies dealing specifically with human rights are set out below. They derive their mandates either from the UN Charter, or from particular human rights treaties.

Commission on Human Rights

The Commission on Human Rights is the most important UN human rights body. It is one of the original six "functional commissions" established by the Economic and Social Council (ECOSOC) in 1946, and reports to the General Assembly through ECOSOC. The Commission has a very broad mandate to discuss any matters relating to human rights. It is an intergovernmental body, composed of 53 states elected for three-year terms on the basis of regional representation (there are five regional groupings in the UN consisting of Asia, Africa, Latin America, Eastern Europe, and Western Europe and Others, which includes Australia, Canada, New Zealand, and the U.S.). Because of the Commission's importance, a great many other UN Member States participate in its work as observers, although they cannot vote. The Commission normally meets for one six-week session each year in Geneva in February and March. Special sessions can be held with the agreement of a majority of members. Recent examples have included special sessions on the situation in former Yugoslavia (in 1992) and the situation in Rwanda (in 1994). The Commission was originally charged with the task of drafting the International Bill of Human Rights, which it has done. In addition, numerous working groups and committees over the years have drafted standards on a wide range of issues. For example, two of the most recently-established working groups will consider possible optional protocols to the Convention on the Rights of the Child. In addition to standard -setting, the Commission reviews recommendations and studies prepared by its subsidiary body, the UN Sub-Commission on the Prevention of Discrimination and Protection of Minorities (see below in this section), and considers and adopts resolutions on general human rights issues and on some specific country situations. Since the Commission generally meets only once each year, it conducts much of its work through its so-called "mechanisms", which focus on a particular theme or on a specific country. A mechanism is merely an individual, usually called a special rapporteur, or a working group, carrying out a certain mandate from the Commission. "Thematic mechanisms", which deal with a certain issue, most relevant to the work of UNHCR include the following:

- Working Group on Enforced or Involuntary Disappearances .
- Special Rapporteur on Torture
- Working Group on Arbitrary Detention
- Special Rapporteur on Extrajudicial, Summary or Arbitrary Executions
- Special Rapporteur on Religious Intolerance
- Special Rapporteur on Violence against Women
- Special Rapporteur on Contemporary Forms of Racism, Racial Discrimination, Xenophobia and Related Intolerance
- Representative of the Secretary-General on Internally Displaced Persons.

There are also, "country-specific mechanisms", nearly all of which are of interest to UNHCR because the country may produce, or already has produced, refugees. Each mechanism has its own mandate, which is contained in the Commission resolution creating it. Generally speaking:

- they examine information and allegations received on the particular subject or country, and "transmit sufficiently documented information and cases to the government -concerned for comment;
- in appropriate cases the government *is* urged to investigate the matter;

- some of the mechanism's have established a procedure for making urgent appeals to the government concerned, for example when reliable information is received on cases Of disappearances or torture;
- with the consent of the government concerned, they can visit a country to observe the situation first-hand; and
- they issue annual reports to the Commission, and in some cases interim reports to the General Assembly, which give a summary of the actions they have taken over the past year and the information they have received, and often include recommendations for improving the situations described. These reports are an extremely useful source of authoritative information on human rights violations in many countries, and are available through the Centre for Documentation on Refugees.

Thematic mechanisms may play a complementary role to actions taken by UNHCR to ensure the protection of asylum seekers and refugees as you can see from the following Excerpt from the Report of the -Special, Rapporteur on Torture to the Commission on Human Rights (1994).

Sub-Commission on the Prevention of Discrimination and Protection of Minorities

The Sub-Commission on the Prevention of Discrimination and Protection of Minorities (often called the Human Rights Sub-Commission or simply the Sub-Commission) was established by and reports to the Commission on Human Rights. The Sub-Commission is composed of 26 members nominated by governments on the basis of regional representation, who are elected to four-year terms by the Commission on Human Rights. The members serve in their individual capacity as independent experts rather than as representatives of their governments. The Sub-Commission's main tasks are to initiate studies on a whole range of human rights questions, not limited to minority or discrimination issues (as with the Commission on Human Rights, these studies are carried out by special rapporteurs or working groups), to adopt resolutions con particular topics or countries, and to make recommendations to the Commission on Human Rights. The Sub-Commission meets for one four-week session each year in August in Geneva.

Treaty Bodies

The "treaty bodies" are expert bodies established by the UN human rights treaties, set up to review the implementation of the treaty. The precise manner in which they do this varies, but generally they are given the competence to review reports submitted by states party to the treaty and to raise questions or concerns about those reports. They may also have the right to receive petitions from individuals alleging a violation of their rights under the treaty. The treaty bodies are implementation control mechanisms with a quasi-judicial function because the reports they publish will contain authoritative views on the scope and content of rights guaranteed in the treaty. The treaty bodies are composed of experts nominated by governments to serve in their personal capacity, not as representative's of their government. Depending on the treaty body, they meet two or three times a year in Geneva, New York and/or Vienna, The main treaty bodies and the conventions they monitor are;

- Committee on the Rights of the Child; Convention on the Rights of the Child,
- Committee against Torture; Convention against Torture.

- Committee on the Elimination of Discrimination against Women; Convention on the Elimination of All Forms of Discrimination against Women.
- Committee on the Elimination of Racial Discrimination: Convention on the Elimination of All Forms of Racial Discrimination.
- Human Rights Committee (not to be confused with the Commission on Human Rights, or, as it is sometimes referred to, the Human Rights Commission, see above in this section); International Covenant on Civil and Political Rights,
- Committee on Economic, Social and Cultural Rights; International Covenant on Economic, Social and Cultural Rights.

Difference between Mechanisms and Treaty Bodies

The mechanisms - working groups and special rapporteurs; - created by the Commission on Human Rights and its Sub-Commission, and the treaty bodies established by human rights treaties are all set up to ensure human rights are respected, The main differences are:

- treaty bodies can deal only with states parties to the treaty, but there is a legal obligation on such states to co-operate with the body; and
- the Commission and Sub-Commission mechanisms can deal with issues within their mandate in any UN Member State, but the legitimacy of their work is occasionally challenged by governments who do not accept their scrutiny,

General Comments of the Treaty Bodies

A number of treaty bodies including the Human Rights Committee, the Committee on Economic, Social and Cultural

Rights, the Committee on the Elimination of racial Discrimination, and the Committee on the Elimination of Discrimination against Women have prepared general comments or recommendations. For example, the Human Rights Committee, under article 40, paragraph 4, of the International Covenant on Civil and Political Rights has authority to study reports submitted by the states parties to the Covenant and transmit its reports, and such general comments as it may consider appropriate, to the states parties. The Committee has to date prepared 24 General Comments on a number of issues such as reporting guidelines, interpretation of specific articles of the Covenant, the use of reservations, and the position of aliens under the Covenant. As concerns the use of these General Comments, the Committee has noted that they can serve to draw the attention of states parties to insufficiencies disclosed by a large number of reports, to suggest improvements in the reporting procedure, and to stimulate activities of these states and international organizations in the promotion and protection of human rights. The Committee has also noted that these Comments should be of interest to other states, especially those preparing to become parties to the Covenant.

High Commissioner for Human Rights

The post of UN High Commissioner for Human Rights was established by the General Assembly in December 1993, following a recommendation made at the World Conference on Human, Rights. The High Commissioner for Human Rights is appointed by the General Assembly on the recommendation of the Secretary- General, and serves for a term of four years with the possibility of one renewal for another four-year term. The High Commissioner for Human Rights is the United Nations' official with principal responsibility for UN human rights activities under the direction and authority of the Secretary- General, and has overall responsibility for the activities of the UN Centre for Human Rights. The High Commissioner for Human Rights has been assigned the role of promoting respect for human rights, coordinating and rationalising the UN human rights programme, making the UN human rights machinery more effective and preventing human rights violations. The establishment of the office of the High Commissioner for Human Rights is significant in that UN human rights activities will be led and coordinated by a senior UN official with a mandate to address all issues of human rights worldwide. In particular, the High Commissioner for Human Rights' preventive function could be of great importance to UNHCR. Moreover, the establishment of this office has led to increased cooperation in post-conflict peace building between UNHCR protection staff and human rights monitors in the field.

Centre for Human Rights

The Centre for Human Rights is a division of the UN Secretariat based in Geneva, It provides legal, technical and administrative support to intergovernmental bodies such as the Commission on Human Rights and its mechanisms, and to the treaty bodies. The Centre prepares studies requested of the Secretary-General on human rights questions, is responsible for dealing with all communications received by the UN on human rights, and operates an advisory services and technical assistance programme on human rights for governments. UNHCR and the Centre cooperate on a number of items of mutual interest, both in Geneva and in the field. UNHCR's refugee law training courses are sometimes undertaken in conjunction with the Centre's advisory services in human rights, and UNHCR field offices often assist visiting special rapporteurs, for example, by facilitating their access to refugees whom they wish to interview about conditions in a country of origin. In the case of the former Yugoslavia, there is a Memorandum of Understanding between UNHCR and the Centre concerning the provision of information on alleged human rights abuses. In addition, UNHCR submits information and views to mechanisms and treaty bodies dealing with issues of concern to the Office. An example of this is the support which UNHCR provides to the Representative of the Secretary-General on Internally Displaced Persons.

Now we will reproduce the text of various important instruments relating to protection of human rights of refugees in the succeeding chapters.

6

Convention Relating to the Status of Refugees

> "When we conquer enemies by kindness and justice we are more apt to win their submission than by victory in the field. In the one case, they yield only to neces-sity; in the other, by their own free choice."
>
> —*Polybius, Histories*

PREAMBLE

The High Contracting Parties

Considering that the Charter of the United Nations and the Universal Declaration of Human Rights approved on 10 December 1948 by the General Assembly have affirmed the principle that human beings shall enjoy fundamental rights and freedoms without discrimination,

Considering that the United Nations has, on various occasions, manifested its profound concern for refugees and endeavoured to assure refugees the widest possible exercise of these fundamental rights and freedoms,

Considering that it is desirable to revise and consolidate previous international agreements relating to the status of refugees and to extend the scope of and the protection accorded by such instruments by means of a new agreement,

Considering that the grant of asylum may place unduly heavy burdens on certain countries, and that a satisfactory solution of a problem of which the United Nations has recognized the international scope and nature cannot therefore be achieved without international co-operation.

Expressing the wish that all States, recognizing the social and humanitarian nature of the problem of refugees, will do everything within their power to prevent this problem from becoming a cause of tension between States.

Noting that the United Nations High Commissioner for Refugees is charged with the task of supervising international conventions providing for the protection of refugees, and recognizing that the effective coordination of measures taken to deal with this problem will depend upon the co-operation of States with the High Commissioner,

Have agreed as follows:

General Provisions

Article 1

Definition of the Term "Refugee"

A. For the purposes of the present Convention, the term "refugee" shall apply to any person who:

(1) Has been considered a refugee under the Arrangements of 12 May 1926 and 30 June 1928 or under the Conventions of 28 October 1933 and 16 February 1938, the Protocol of 14 September 1939 or the Constitution of the International Refugee Organization;

Decisions of non-eligibility taken by the International Refugee Organization during the period of its activities shall not prevent the status of refugee being accorded to persons who fulfil the conditions of paragraph 2 of this section;

(2) As a result of events occurring before I January 1951 and owing to well-founded fear of being persecuted for reasons of race, religion, nationality, membership of a particular social group or political opinion, is outside the country of his nationality and is unable or, owing to such fear, is unwilling to avail himself of the protection of that country; or who, not having a nationality and being outside the country of his former habitual residence as a result of such events, is unable or owing to such fear, is unwilling to return to it.

In the case of a person who has more than one nationality, the term, "the country of his nationality" shall mean each of the countries of which he is a national and a person shall not be deemed to be lacking the protection of the country of his nationality if, without any valid reason based on well-founded fear, he has not availed himself of the protection of one of the countries of which he is a national.

B. (1) For the purposes of this Convention, the words "events occurring before 1 January 1951" in Article 1, Section A, shall be understood to mean either

(a) "events occurring in Europe before I January 1951" or

(b) "events occurring in Europe or elsewhere before I January 1951", and each Contracting State shall make a declaration at the time of signature, ratification or accession, specifying which of these meanings it applies for the purpose of its obligations under this Convention.

(2) Any Contracting State which has adopted alternative (a) may at any time extend its obligations by adopting alternative (b) by means of a notification addressed to the Secretary-General of tile United Nations.

C. This Convention shall cease to apply to any person falling under the terms of section A if:

(1) He has voluntarily re-availed himself of the protection of the country of his nationality; or

(2) Having lost his nationality, he has voluntarily re-acquired it; or

(3) He has acquired a new nationality, and enjoys the protection of the country of his new nationality; or

(4) He has voluntarily re-established himself in the country which he left or outside which he remained owing to fear of persecution; or

(5) He can no longer, because the circumstances in connexion with which he has been recognized as a refugee have ceased to exist, continue to refuse to avail himself of the protection of the country of his nationality;

Provided that this paragraph shall not apply to a refugee, falling under section A (1) of this Article who is able to invoke compelling reasons rising out of previous persecution for refusing to avail himself of the protection of the country of nationality;

(6) Being a person who has no nationality he is, because the circumstances in connexion with

which he has been recognized as a refugee have ceased to exist, able to return to the country of his , former habitual residence.

Provide that this paragraph shall not apply to a refugee falling under section A (1) of this Article who is able to invoke to compelling reasons arising out of previous persecution for refusing to return to the country of his former habitual residence,

D. This Convention shall not apply to persons who are, at present receiving from organs or agencies of the United Nations: other than the United Nations High Commissioner for Refugees protection, or assistance.

When such protection or assistance has ceased for any reason, without the position of such persons being definitively settled in accordance with the relevant resolutions adopted by the General Assembly of the United Nations, these persons shall ipso facto be entitled to the benefits of this Convention,

E. This Convention shall not apply to a person who is recognized by the competent authorities of the country in which he has taken residence as having the rights and obligations which are attached to the possession of the nationality of that country.

F. The provisions of this Convention shall not apply to any person with respect to whom there are serious reasons for considering that:

(a) he has committed a crime against peace, a war crime, or a crime against humanity, as defined in the international instruments drawn up to make provision in respect of such crimes;

(b) he has committed a serious non-political crime

outside the country of refuge prior to his admission to that country as a refugee;

(c) he has been guilty of acts contrary to the purposes and principles of the United Nations,

Article 2

General Obligations

Every refugee is duties to the country in which he finds himself, which require in particular that he conform to its laws and regulations as well as to measures taken for the maintenance of public order.

Article 3

Non-discrimination

The Contracting States shall apply the provisions of this Convention to refugees without discrimination as to race, religion or country of origin.

Article 4

Religion

The Contracting States shall accord to refugees within their territories treatment at least as favourable as that accorded to their nationals with respect, to freedom to practise their religion and freedom as regards the religious education of their children.

Article 5

Rights Granted Apart from This Convention

Nothing in this Convention shall be deemed to impair any rights and benefits granted by a Contracting State to refugees apart from this Convention,

Article 6

The Term "in the Same Circumstances"

For the purpose of this Convention, the term "in the

same circumstances" implies that any requirements (including requirements as to length and conditions of sojourn or residence) which the particular individual would have to fulfil for the enjoyment of the right in question, if he were not a refugee, must be fulfilled by him, with the exception of requirements which by their nature a refugee is incapable of fulfilling.

Article 7

Exemption from Reciprocity

1. Except where this Convention contains more favourable provisions, a Contracting State shall accord to refugees the same treatment as is accorded to aliens generally.
2. After a period of three years' residence, all refugees shall enjoy exemption from legislative reciprocity in the territory of the Contracting States.
3. Each Contracting State shall continue to accord to refugees the rights and benefits to which they were already entitled, in the absence of reciprocity, at the date of entry into force of this Convention for that State,
4. The Contracting States shall consider favourably, the possibility of according to refugees, in the absence of reciprocity, rights and benefits beyond those to which they are entitled according to paragraphs 2, and 3, and to extending exemption from reciprocity to refugee's who do not fulfil the conditions provided for in paragraphs 2 and 3.
5. The provisions of paragraphs 2 and 3 apply both to the rights and benefits referred to in Articles 13, 18, 19, 21 and 22 of this Convention and to rights and benefits for which this Convention does not provide,

Article 8

Exemption from Exceptional Measures

With regard to exceptional measures which may be taken against the person, property or interests of nationals of a foreign State, the Contracting States shall not apply such measures to a refugee who is formally a national of the said State solely on account of such nationality. Contracting States which, under their legislation, are prevented from applying the general principle expressed in this Article shall, in appropriate cases, pant exemptions in favour of such refugees.

Article 9

Provisional Measures

Nothing in this Convention shall prevent a Contracting State, in time of war or other grave and exceptional circumstances, from taking provisionally measures which it considers to be essential to the national security in the case of a particular person, pending a determination by the Contracting State that person is in fact a refugee and that the continuance of such measures is necessary in his case in the interests of national security,

Article 10

Continuity of Residence

1. Where a refugee has been forcibly displaced during the Second World War and removed to the territory of a Contracting State, and is resident there, the period of such enforced sojourn shall be considered to have been lawful residence within that territory,
2. Where a refugee has been forcibly displaced during the Second World War from the territory of a Contracting State and has, prior to the date of entry

into force of this Convention, returned there for the purpose of taking up residence, the period of residence before and after such enforced displacement shall be regarded as one uninterrupted period for any purposes for which uninterrupted residence is required.

Article 11

Refugee Seamen

In the case of refugees regularly serving as crew members on board a ship flying the flag of a Contracting State, that State shall give sympathetic consideration to their establishment on its territory and the issue of travel documents to them or their temporary admission to its territory particularly with a view to facilitating their establishment in another country.

Juridical Status

Article 12

Personal Status

1. The personal status of a refugee shall be governed by the law of the country of his domicile or, if hi has no domicile, by the law-of the country of his residence,
2. Rights previously acquired by a refugee and dependent on personal status, more particularly rights attaching to marriage, shall be respected by a Contracting State, subject to compliance, if this be necessary, with the formalities required by the law of that State, provided that the right in question is one which would have been recognized by the law of that State had he not become a refugee,

Article 13

Movable and Immovable Property

The Contracting States shall accord to a refugee treatment

as favourable as possible and, in any event, not less favourable than that accorded to aliens generally in the same circumstances, as regards the acquisition of movable and immovable property and other rights pertaining thereto, and to leases and other contracts relating to movable and immovable property.

Article 14

Artistic Rights and Industrial Property

In respect of the protection of industrial property, such as inventions', designs or models, trade marks, trade names, and of rights in literary, artistic and scientific works, a refugee shall be accorded in, the country in which he has his habitual residence the same protection as is accorded to nationals of that country. In the territory of any other Contracting State, he shall be accorded the same protection as is accorded in that territory to nationals of the country in which he has his habitual residence,

Article 15

Right of Association

As regards non-political and non-profit- making associations and trade unions the Contracting States shall accord to refugees lawfully staying in their territory the most favourable treatment accorded to nationals of a reign country, in the same circumstances.

Article 16

Access to Courts

1. A refugee shall have free access to the courts of law on the territory of 11 Contracting States,
2. A refugee shall enjoy in the Contracting State in which he has his habitual residence the same treatment as a national in matters pertaining to access to the

Courts, including legal assistance and exemption from cautio judicatum solvi.

3. A refugee shall be accorded in the matters referred to in paragraph 2 in countries other than that in which he has his habitual residence the treatment granted to a national of the country of his habitual residence.

Gainful Employments

Article 17

Wage-Earning Employment

1. The Contracting State shall accord to refugees lawfully staying in their territory the most favourable treatment accorded to nationals of a foreign country in the same circumstances, as regards the right to enrage in wage-earning employment.
2. In any case, restrictive measures imposed on aliens or the employment aliens for the protection of the national labour market shall not be applied to a refugee who was already exempt from them at the date of entry not force of this Convention for the Contracting State concerned, or who fulfils one of the following conditions:
   (a) He has completed three years' residence in the country,
   (b) He has a spouse possessing the nationality of the country of residence. A refugee may not invoke the benefits of this provision if he has abandoned his spouse,
   (c) He has one or more children possessing the nationality of the country of residence.

Article 18

Self-employment

The Contracting States shall accord to a refugee lawfully

in their territory treatment as favourable as possible and, in any event, not less favourable than that accorded to aliens generally in the same circumstances, as regards the right to engage on his own account in agriculture, industry, handicrafts and commerce and to establish commercial and industrial companies.

Article 19

Liberal Professions

1. Each Contracting State shall accord to refugees lawfully staying in their territory who hold diplomas recognized by the competent authorities of that State, and who are desirous of practising a liberal profession, treatment as favourable as possible and, in any event, not less favourable than that accorded to aliens generally in thc samc circumstances.
2. The; Contracting States shall use their best endeavours consistently with their laws and constitutions to secure the settlement of such refugees in the territories, other than the metropolitan territory, for whose international relations they are responsible.

Welfare

Article 20

Rationing

Where a rationing system exists, which applies to the population at large and regulates the general distribution of products in short supply, refugees shall be accorded the same treatment as nationals.

Article 21

Housing

As regards housing, the Contracting States, in so far as

the matter is regulated by laws or regulations or is subject to the control of public authorities, shall accord to refugees lawfully staying in their territory treatment as favourable as possible and, in any event, not less favourable than that accorded to aliens generally in the same circumstances.

Article 22

Public Education

1. The Contracting States shall accord to refugees the same treatment as is accorded to nationals with respect to elementary education.
2. The Contracting States shall accord to refugees treatment as favourable as possible, and, in any event, not less favourable than that accorded to aliens generally in the same circumstances, with respect to education other than elementary education and, in particular, as regards access to studies, the recognition of foreign school certificates, diplomas and degrees, the remission of fees and charges and the award of scholarships.

Article 23

Public Relief

The Contracting States shall accord to refugees lawfully staying in their territory the same treatment with respect to public relief and assistance as is accorded to their nationals.

Article 24

Labour Legislation and Social Security

1. The Contracting States shall accord to refugees lawfully staying in their territory the same treatment as is accorded to nationals in respect of the following matters:

(a) In so far as such matters are governed by laws or regulations or are subject to the control of administrative authorities: remuneration, including family allowances where these form part of, remuneration, hours of work, overtime arrangements, holidays with pay, restrictions on home work, minimum age of employment, apprenticeship and training, women's work and the work of young persons, and the enjoyment of the benefits of collective bargaining;

(b) Social security (legal provisions in respect of employment injury, occupational diseases, maternity, sickness, disability, old *age,* death, unemployment, family responsibilities and any other contingency which, according to national laws or regulations, is covered by a social security scheme), subject to the following limitations:

(i) There may be appropriate arrangements for the maintenance of acquired rights and rights in course of acquisition;

(ii) National laws or regulations of the country of residence may prescribe special arrangements concerning benefits or portions of benefits which are payable wholly out of public funds, and concerning allowances paid to persons who do not fulfil the contribution conditions prescribed for the award of a normal pension.

2. The right to compensation for the death of a refugee resulting from employment injury or from occupational disease shall not be affected by the fact

that the residence of the beneficiary is outside the territory of the Contracting State.

3. The Contracting States shall extend to refugees the benefits of agreements concluded between them, or which may be concluded between them in the future, concerning the maintenance of acquired rights and rights in the process of acquisition in regard to social security, subject only to the conditions which apply to nationals of the States signatory to the agreements in question.
4. The Contracting States will give sympathetic consideration to extending to refugees so far as possible the benefits of similar agreements which may at any time be in force between such Contracting States and non-contracting States.

Administrative Measures

Article 25

Administrative Assistance

1. When the exercise of a right by a refugee would normally require the assistance of authorities of a foreign country to whom he cannot have recourse, the Contracting States in whose territory he is residing shall arrange that such assistance be afforded to him by their own authorities or by an international authority.
2. The authority or authorities mentioned in paragraph I shall deliver or cause to be delivered under their supervision to refugees such documents or certifications as would normally be delivered to aliens by or through their national authorities.
3. Documents or certifications so delivered shall stand in the stead of the official instruments delivered to

aliens by or through their national authorities, and shall be given credence in the absence of proof to the contrary.

4. Subject to such exceptional treatment as may be granted to indigent persons, fees may be charged for the services mentioned herein, but such fees shall be moderate and commensurate with those charged to nationals for similar services.
5. The provisions of this Article shall be without prejudice to Articles 27 and 28.

Article 26

Freedom of Movement

Each Contracting State shall accord to refugees lawfully in its territory the right to choose their place of residence and to move freely within its territory, subject to any regulations applicable to aliens generally in the same circumstances.

Article 27

Identity Papers

The Contracting States shall issue identity papers to any refugee in their territory who does not possess a valid travel document.

Article 28

Travel Documents

1. The Contracting States shall issue to refugees lawfully staying in their territory travel documents for the purpose of travel outside their territory unless compelling reasons of national security or public order otherwise require, and the provisions of the Schedule to this Convention shall apply with respect

to such documents. The Contracting States may issue such a travel document to any other refugee in their territory, they shall in particular give sympathetic consideration to the issue of such a travel document to refugees in their territory who are unable to obtain a travel document from the country of their lawful residence.

2. Travel documents issued to refugees under previous international agreements by parties thereto shall be recognized and treated by the Contracting States in the same way as if they had been issued pursuant to this Article.

Article 29

Fiscal Charges

1. The Contracting States shall not impose upon refugees duties, charges or taxes, of any description whatsoever, other or higher than those which are or may be levied on their nationals in similar situations.
2. Nothing in the above paragraph shall prevent the application to refugees of the laws and regulations concerning charges in respect of the issue to aliens of administrative documents including identity papers.

Article 30

Transfer of Assets

1. A Contracting State shall, in conformity with its laws and regulations, permit refugees to transfer assets which they have brought into its territory to another country where they have been admitted for the purposes of resettlement,
2. A Contracting State shall give sympathetic consideration to the application of refugees for

permission to transfer assets wherever they may be and which are necessary for their resettlement in another country to which they have been admitted,

Article 31

Refugees Unlawfully in the Country of Refuge

1. The Contracting States shall not impose penalties, on account of their illegal entry or presence, on refugees who, coining directly from a territory where their life or freedom was threatened in the sense of Article 1, enter or are present in their territory without authorization, provided they present themselves without delay to the authorities and show good cause for their illegal entry or presence,
2. The Contracting States shall not apply to the movements of such refugees restrictions other than those which are necessary and such restrictions shall only be applied until their status in the country is regularized or they obtain admission into another country, The Contracting States shall allow such refugees a reasonable period and all the necessary facilities to obtain admission into another country.

Article 32

Expulsion

1. The Contracting States shall not expel a refugee lawfully in their territory save on grounds of national security or public order.
2. The expulsion of such a refugee shall be only in pursuance of a decision reached in accordance with due process of law. Except where compelling reasons of national security otherwise require, the refugee shall be allowed to submit evidence to clear himself,

and to appeal to and be represented for the purpose before competent authority or a person or persons specially designated by the competent authority.

3. The Contracting States shall allow such a refugee a reasonable period within which to seek legal admission into another country. The Contracting States reserve the fight to apply during that period such internal measures as they may deem necessary,

Article 33

Prohibition of Expulsion or Return ("Refoulement")

1. No Contracting State shall expel or return ("refouler") a refugee in any manner whatsoever to the frontiers of territories where his life or freedom would be threatened on account of his race, religion, nationality, membership of a particular social group or political opinion.
2. The benefit of the present provision may not, however, be claimed by a refugee whom there are reasonable grounds for regarding as a danger to the security of the country in which he is, or who, having been convicted by a final judgment of a particularly serious crime, constitutes a danger to the community of that country.

Article 34

Naturalization

The Contracting States shall as far as possible facilitate the assimilation and naturalization of refugees. They shall in particular make every effort to expedite naturalization proceedings and to reduce as far as possible the charges and costs of such proceedings.

Executory and Transitory Provisions

Article 35

Co-operation of the National Authorities with the United Nations

1. The Contracting States undertake to co-operate with the Office of the United Nations High Commissioner for Refugees, or any other agency of the United Nations which may succeed it, in the exercise of its functions, and shall in particular facilitate its duty of supervising the application of the provisions of this Convention.
2. In order to enable the Office of the High Commissioner, or any other agency of the United Nations which may succeed it, to make reports to the competent organs of the United Nations, the Contracting States undertake to provide them in the appropriate form with information and statistical data requested concerning:
   (a) the condition of refugees,
   (b) the implementation of this Convention, and
   (c) laws, regulations and decrees which are, or may hereafter be, in force relating to refugees.

Article 36

Information on National Legislation

The Contracting States shall communicate to the Secretary-General of the United Nations the laws and regulations which they may adopt to ensure the application of this Convention.

Article 37

Relation to Previous Conventions

Without prejudice to Article 28, paragraph 2, of this

Convention, this Convention replaces, as between parties to it, the Arrangements of 5 July 1922, 31 May 1924, 12 May 1926, 30 June 1928 and 30 July 1935, the Conventions of 28 October 1933 and 10 February 1938, the Protocol of 14 September 1939 and the Agreement of 15 October 1946.

Final Clauses

Article 38

Settlement of Disputes

Any dispute between parties to this Convention relating to its interpretation or application, which cannot be settled by other means, shall be referred to the International Court of Justice at the request of any one of the parties to the dispute.

Article 39

Signature, Ratification and Accession

1. This Convention shall be opened for signature at Geneva on 28 July 1951 and shall thereafter be deposited with the Secretary-General of the United Nations. It shall be open for signature at the European Office of the United Nations from 28 July to 31 August 1951 and shall be re-opened for signature at the Headquarters of the United Nations from 17 September 1951 to 31 December 1952.
2. This Convention shall be open for signature on behalf of all States Members of the United Nations, and also on behalf of any other State invited to attend the Conference of Plenipotentiaries on the Status of Refugees and Stateless Persons or to which an invitation to sign will have been addressed by the General Assembly. It shall be ratified and the instruments of ratification shall be deposited with the Secretary-General of the United Nations.

3. This Convention shall be open from 28 July 1951 for accession by the States referred to in paragraph 2 of this Article. Accession shall be effected by the deposit of an instrument of accession with the Secretary - General of the United Nations.

Article 40

Territorial Application Clause

1. Any State may, at the time of signature, ratification or accession declare that this Convention shall extend to all or any of the territories for the international relations of which it is responsible. Such a declaration shall take effect when the Convention enters into force for the State concerned.
2. At any time thereafter any such extension shall be made by notification addressed to the Secretary - General of the United Nations and shall take effect as from the ninetieth day after the day of receipt by the Secretary-General of the United Nations of this notification, or as from the date of entry into force of the Convention for the State concerned, whichever is the later.
3. With respect to those territories to which this Convention is not extended at the time of signature, ratification or accession,- each State concerned shall consider the possibility of taking the necessary steps in order to extend the application of this Convention to such territories, subject, where necessary for constitutional reasons, to the consent of the governments of such territories

Article 41

Federal Clause

In the case of a Federal or non-unitary State, the following provisions shall apply:

(a) With respect to those Articles of this Convention that come within the legislative jurisdiction of the federal legislative authority, the obligations of the Federal Government shall to this extent be the same as those of Parties which are not Federal States.

(b) With respect to those Articles of this Convention that come within the legislative jurisdiction of constituent States, provinces or cantons which are not, under the constitutional system of the federation, bound to take legislative action, the Federal Government shall bring such Articles with a favourable recommendation to the notice of the appropriate authorities of States, provinces or cantons at the earliest possible moment,

(c) A Federal State Party to this Convention shall, at the request of any other Contracting State transmitted through the Secretary -General of the United Nations, supply a statement of the law and practice of the Federation and its constituent units in regard to any particular provision of the Convention showing the extent to which effect has been given to that provision by legislative or other action,

Article 42
Reservations

1. At the time of signature, ratification or accession, any State may make reservations to Articles of the Convention other than to Articles 1, 3, 4 16 (1), 33, 36-46 inclusive.

2. Any State making a reservation in accordance with paragraph I of the Article may at any time withdraw the reservation by a communication to that effect addressed to the Secretary-General of the United Nations.

Article 43

Entry into Force

1. This Convention shall come into force on the ninetieth day following the day of deposit of the sixth instrument of ratification or accession.
2. For each State ratifying or acceding to the Convention after the deposit of the sixth instrument of ratification or accession' the Convention shall enter into force on the ninetieth day following the date of deposit by such State of its instrument of ratification or accession,

Article 44

Denunciation

1. Any Contracting State may denounce this Convention at any time by a notification addressed to the Secretary-General of the United Nations.
2. Such denunciation shall take effect for the Contracting State concerned one year from the date upon which it is received by the Secretary-General of the United Nations,
3. Any State which has made a declaration or notification under Article 40 may, at any, time thereafter, by a notification to the Secretary-General of the United Nations, declare that the Convention shall cease to extend to such territory one year after the date of receipt of the notification by the Secretary-General,

Article 45

Revision

1. Any Contracting State may request revision of this Convention at an time by a notification addressed to the Secretary-General of the Unite Nations,

2. The General Assembly of the United Nations shall recommend the steps, if any to be taken in respect of such request.

Article 46

Notifications by the Secretary-General of the United Nations

The Secretary-General of the United Nations shall inform all Members of the United Nations and non-member States referred to in Article 39:

(a) of declarations and notifications in accordance with Section B of Article 1;

(b) of signature, ratifications and accessions in accordance with Article 39;

(c) of declarations and notifications in accordance with Article 40;

(d) of reservations and withdrawals in accordance with Article 42;

(e) of the date on which this Convention will come into force in accordance with Article 43;

(f) of denunciations and notifications in accordance with Article 44;

(g) of requests for revision in accordance with Article 45.

IN FAITH WHEREOF the undersigned, duly authorized, have signed this Convention on behalf of their respective Governments.

DONE at Geneva, this twenty-eighth day of July, one thousand nine hundred and fifty-one, in a single copy, of which the English and French texts are equally authentic and which shall remain deposited in the archives of the

United Nations, and certified true copies of which shall be delivered to all Members of the United Nations and to the non-member States referred to in Article 39.

Schedule

Paragraph 1

1. The travel document, referred to in Article 28 of this Convention shall be similar to the specimen annexed hereto.
2. The document shall be made out in at least two languages, one of which shall be English or French.

Paragraph 2

Subject to the regulations obtaining in the country of issue, children may be included in the travel document of a parent or, in exceptional circumstances, of another adult refugee.

Paragraph 3

The fees charged for issue of the document shall not exceed the lowest scale of charges for national passports.

Paragraph 4

Save in special or exceptional cases, the document shall be made valid for the largest possible number of countries.

Paragraph 5

The document shall have a validity of either one or two years, at the discretion of the issuing authority.

Paragraph 6

1. The renewal or extension of the validity of the document is a matter for the authority which issued it, so long as the holder has not established lawful

residence in another territory and resides lawfully in the territory of the said authority. The issue of a new document is, under the same conditions, a matter for the authority which issued the former document.

2. Diplomatic or consular authorities, specially authorized for the purpose, shall be empowered to extend, for a period not, exceeding six months, the validity of travel documents issued by their Governments.
3. The Contracting States shall give sympathetic consideration to renewing or extending the validity of travel documents or issuing new documents to refugees no longer lawfully resident in their territory who are unable to obtain a travel document from the country of their lawful residence.

Paragraph 7

The Contracting States shall recognize the validity of the documents issued in accordance with the provisions of Article 28 of this Convention.

Paragraph 8

The competent authorities of the country to which the refugee desires to proceed shall, if they are prepared to admit him and if a visa is required, affix a visa on the document of which he is the holder.

Paragraph 9

1. The Contracting States undertake to issue transit visas to refugees who have obtained visas for a territory of final destination.
2. The issue of such visas 'may be refused on grounds which would justify refusal of a visa to any alien.

Paragraph 10

The fees for the issue of exit, entry or transit visas shall not exceed the lowest scale of charges for visas on foreign passports.

Paragraph 11

When a refugee has lawfully taken up residence in the territory of another Contracting State, the responsibility for the issue of a new document, under the terms and conditions of Article 28, shall be that of the competent authority of that territory, to which the refugee shall be entitled to apply.

Paragraph 12

The authority issuing a new document shall withdraw the old document and shall return it to the country of issue, if it is stated in the document that it should be so returned; otherwise it shall withdraw and cancel the document.

Paragraph 13

1. Each Contracting State undertakes that the holder of a travel document issued by it in accordance with Article 28 of this Convention shall be readmitted to its territory at any time during the period of its validity.
2. Subject to the provisions of the preceding subparagraph, a Contracting State may require the holder of the document to comply with such formalities as may be prescribed in regard to exit from or return to its territory.
3. The Contracting States reserve the right, in exceptional eases, or in cases where the refugee's stay is authorized for a specific period, when issuing the document, to limit the period during which the refugee may return to a period of not less than three months.

Paragraph 14

Subject only to the terms of paragraph 13, the provisions of this Schedule in no way affect the laws and regulations governing the conditions of admission to, transit through, residence and establishment in, and departure from, the territories of the Contracting States,

Paragraph 15

Neither the issue of the document nor the entries made thereon determine or affect the status of the holder, particularly as regards nationality,

Paragraph 16

The issue of the document does not in any way entitle the holder to the protection of the diplomatic or consular authorities of the country of issue, and does not confer on these authorities a right of protection.

ANNEX

Specimen Travel Document

The document will be in booklet form (approximately 15 x 10 centimetres).

It is recommended that it be so printed that any erasure or alteration by chemical or other means can be readily detected, and that the words "Convention of 28 July 1951" be printed in continuous repetition on each page, in the language of the issuing country.

TRAVEL DOCUMENT

(Convention of 28 July 1951)

7

Protocol Relating to Status of Refugees (1967)

"The extraordinary thing about my father is that his public face and his private face have been the same. He has been the same man to the world that he has been to his family. And that is harder than it sounds. It is the very definition of integrity."

—*Charles Van Doren*

The States Parties to the Present Protocol

Considering that the Convention relating to the Status of Refugees done at Geneva on 28 July 1951 (hereinafter referred to as the Convention) covers only those persona who have become refugees as a result of events occurring before I January 1951,

Considering that new refugee situations have arisen since the Convention was adopted and that the refugees concerned may therefore not fall within the scope of the Convention,

Considering that it is desirable that equal status Should be enjoyed by all refugees covered by the definition in the Convention irrespective of the dateline I January 1951,

Have agreed as follows:

Article I

General Provision

1. The States Parties to the present Protocol undertake to apply Articles 2 to 84 inclusive of the Convention to refugees as hereinafter defined.
2. For the purpose of the present Protocol, the term "refugee" shall, except as regards the application of paragraph 8 of this Article, mean any person within the definition of Article 1 of the Convention as if the words "As a result of events occurring before 1 January 1951 and ..." and the words as a result of such events", in Article I A (2) were omitted.
3. The present Protocol shall be applied by the States Parties hereto without any geographic limitation, save that existing declarations made by States already Parties to the Convention in accordance with Article I B (1) (a) of the Convention shall, unless extended under Article I B (2) thereof, apply also under the present Protocol.

Article II

Co-operation of the National Authorities with the United Nations

1. The States Parties to the present Protocol undertake to co-operate with the Office of the United Nations High Commissioner for Refugees, or any other agency of the United Nations which may succeed it, in the exercise of its functions, and shall in particular facilitate its duty of supervising the application of the provisions of the present Protocol.
2. In order to enable the Office of the High Commissioner, or any other agency of the United Nations which may succeed it, to make reports to the competent organs of the United Nations, the States Parties to

the present Protocol undertake to provide them with the information and statistical data requested, in the appropriate form, concerning:

(a) The condition of refugees;

(b) The implementation of the present Protocol;

(c) Laws, regulations and decrees which are, or - may hereafter be, in force relating to refugees.

Article III

Information on National Legislation

The States Parties to the present Protocol shall communicate to the Secretary-General of the United Nations the laws and regulations which they may adopt to ensure the application of the present Protocol.

Article IV

Settlement of Disputes

Any dispute between States Parties to the present Protocol- which relates to its interpretation or application and which cannot be settled by other means shall be referred to the International Court of Justice at the request of any one of the parties to the dispute.

Article V

Accession

The present Protocol shall be open for accession on behalf of all States Parties to the Convention and of any other State Member of the United Nations or member of any of the specialized agencies or to which an invitation to accede may have been addressed by the General Assembly of the United Nations. Accession shall be effected by the deposit of an instrument of accession with the Secretary -General of the United Nations.

Article VI

Federal Clause

In the case of a Federal or non-unitary State, the following provisions shall apply:

(a) With respect to those articles of the Convention to be applied in accordance with Article 1, paragraph 1, of the present Protocol that come within the legislative jurisdiction of the federal legislative authority, the obligations of the Federal Government shall to this extent be the same as those of States-Parties which are not Federal States;

(b) With respect to those articles of the Convention to be applied in accordance with Article 1, paragraph 1, of the present Protocol that come within the legislative jurisdiction of constituent States, provinces or cantons which are not, under the constitutional system of the Federation, bound to take legislative action, the Federal Government shall bring such articles with a favourable recommendation to the notice of the appropriate authorities of States, provinces or cantons at the earliest possible moment;

(c) A Federal State Party to the present Protocol shall, at the request of any other State Party hereto transmitted through the Secretary-General of the United Nations, supply a statement of the law and practice of the Federation and its constituent units in regard to any particular provision of the Convention to be applied in accordance with Article 1, paragraph 1, of the present Protocol, showing the extent to which effect has been given to that provision by legislative or other action,

Article VII

Reservations and Declarations

1. At the time of accession, any State may make reservations in respect of Article IV of the present Protocol and in respect of the application in accordance with Article I of the present Protocol of any provisions of the Convention other than those contained in Articles 1, 3, 4, 16 (1) and 33 thereof, provided that in the case of a State Party to the Convention reservations made under tin's Article shall not extend to refugees in respect of whom the Convention applies.
2. Reservations made by States Parties to the Convention in accordance with Article 42 thereof shall, unless withdrawn, be applicable in relation to their obligations under the present Protocol,
3. Any State making a reservation in accordance with paragraph 1 of this Article may at any time withdraw such reservation by a communication to that effect addressed to the Secretary-General of the United Nations.
4. Declarations made under Article 40, paragraphs 1 and 2, of the Convention by a State Party thereto which accedes to the present, Protocol shall be deemed to apply in respect of the present Protocol, unless upon accession a notification to the contrary is addressed by the State Party concerned to the Secretary-General of the United Nations. The provisions of Article 40, paragraphs 2 and 3, and of Article 44, paragraph 3, of the Convention shall be deemed to apply mutatis mutandis to the present Protocol.

Article VIII

Entry into Force

1. The present Protocol shall come into force on the day of deposit of the sixth instrument of accession.
2. For each State acceding to the Protocol after the deposit of the sixth instrument of accession, the Protocol shall come into force on the date of deposit by such State of its instrument of accession.

Article IX

Denunciation

1. Any State Party hereto may denounce this Protocol at any time by a notification addressed to the Secretary -General of the United Nations.
2. Such denunciation shall take effect, for the State Party concerned one year from the date on which it is received by the' Secretary-General of the United Nations,

Article X

Notifications by the Secretary -General of the United-Nations

The Secretary -General of the United Nations shall Inform the States referred to in Article V above of date of entry into force, accessions, reservations and withdrawals of reservations to and denunciations of the present Protocol, and of declarations and notifications relating hereto,

Article XI

Deposit in the Archives of the Secretariat of the United Nations

A copy of the present Protocol, of which the Chinese, English, French, Russian and Spanish texts are equally authentic, signed by the President of the General Assembly and by the Secretary-General of the United Nations, shall be deposited in the archives of the Secretariat of the United Nations, The Secretary-General will transmit certified copies thereof to all States Members of the United Nations and to the other States referred to in Article V above,

APPENDIX

GENERAL ASSEMBLY RESOLUTION 2198 (XXI)

Protocol relating to the Status of Refugees

The General Assembly,

Considering that the Convention relating to the Status of Refugees, signed at Geneva on 28 July 1951, covers only those persons who have become refugees as a result of events occurring before 1 January 1951,

Considering that new refugee situations have arisen since the Convention was adopted and that the refugees concerned may therefore not fall within the scope of the Convention,

Considering that it is desirable that equal status should be enjoyed by all refugees covered by the definition in the Convention, irrespective of the date-line of 1 January 1951,

Taking note of the recommendation of the Executive Committee of the Programme of the United Nations High Commissioner for Refugees that the draft Protocol relating to the Status of Refugees should be submitted to the General Assembly after consideration by the Economic and Social and General Assembly after consideration by the Economic and Social Council, in order that the Secretary-General might be authorised to open the Protocol for accession-by Governments within the shortest possible time,

Considering that the Economic and Social Council in its resolution 1186 (XLI) of 18 November 1966, took note with approval of the draft Protocol contained in the addendum to the report of the United Nations High Commissioner for Refugees and concerning measures to extend the personal scope of the Convention and transmitted the addendum to the General Assembly,

1. *Takes note* of the Protocol relating to the Status of Refugees, the text of which is contained in the addendum to the report of the United Nations High Commissioner for Refugees;
2. *Requests* the Secretary-General to transmit the text of the Protocol to the States mentioned in article V thereof, with a view to enabling them to accede to the Protocol.

8

Constitution of International Refugee Organization

> "Most controversies would soon be ended, if those engaged in them would first accurately define their terms, and then adhere to their definitions."
>
> — *Tyron Edwards*

Preamble

The Governments accepting this Constitution,

Recognizing:

that genuine refugees and displaced persons constitute an urgent problem which is international in scope and character;

that as regards displaced persons, the main task to be performed is to courage and assist in every way possible their early return, to their country of origin;

that genuine refugees and displaced persons should be assisted by international action, either to return to their countries of nationality or former habitual residence, or to find new homes elsewhere under the conditions provided for in this Constitution; or in the case of Spanish Republicans, to establish themselves temporarily in order to enable them to return to Spain when the present Falangist regime is succeeded by a democratic regime;

that re-settlement and re-establishment of refugees and displaced persons be contemplated only in cases indicated clearly in the Constitution;

that genuine refugees and displaced persons, until such time as their repatriation or re-settlement and re-establishment is effectively completed, should be protected in their rights and legitimate interests, should receive care and assistance and, as far as possible, should be put to useful employment, in order to avoid the evil and anti-social consequences of continued idleness; and

that the expenses of repatriation to the extent practicable should be charged to Germany and Japan for persons displaced by those Powers from countries occupied by them: we agreed:

Have Agreed:

the accomplishment of the foregoing purposes in the shortest possible time, to establish and do hereby establish, a non-permanent organization to be called the International Refugee Organization, a specialized agency to be brought into relationship with the United Nations, and accordingly

Have accepted the following articles:

Article 1

Mandate

The mandate of the Organization shall extend to refugees and displaced persons in accordance with the principles, definitions and conditions set forth in Annex I, which is attached to and made an integral part of this Constitution.

Article 2

Functions and Powers

1. The functions of the Organization to be carried out in accordance with the purposes and the principles

of the Charter of the United Nations shall be: the repatriation; the identification, registration and classification; the care and assistance; the legal and political protection; the transport; and the re-settlement and re-establishment, in countries able and willing to receive them, of persons who are the concern of the Organization under the provisions of Annex 1. Such functions shall be exercised with a view:

(a) to encouraging and assisting in every way possible the early return to their country of nationality, or former habitual residence, of those persons who are the concern of the Organization, having regard to the principles laid down in the resolution on refugees and displaced persons adopted by the General Assembly of the United Nations on 1 February 1946 (Annex 111) and to the principles set forth in the Preamble, and to promoting this by all possible means, in particular by providing them with material assistance, adequate food-for a period of three months from the time of their departure from their present places of residence provided they are returning to a country suffering as a result of enemy occupation during the war, and provided such food shall be distributed under the auspices of the Organization; and the necessary clothing and means of transportation; and

(b) with respect to persons for whom repatriation does not take place under paragraph I (a) of this article to facilitating:

(i) their re-establishment in countries of temporary residence;

(ii) the emigration to, re-settlement and re-establishment in other countries of individuals or family units; and

(iii) as may be necessary and practicable, within available resources and subject to the relevant financial regulations, the investigation, promotion or execution of projects of group re-settlement or large-scale re-settlement.

(c) with respect to Spanish Republicans to assisting them to establish themselves temporarily until the time when a democratic regime in Spain is established.

2. For the purpose of carrying out its functions, the Organization may engage in all appropriate activities and, to this end, shall have power:

(a) to receive and disburse private and public funds;

(b) as necessary to acquire land and buildings by lease, gift, or in exceptional circumstances only, by purchase; and to hold such land and buildings or to dispose of them by lease, sale or otherwise;

(c) to acquire, hold and convey other necessary property;

(d) to enter into contracts, and undertake obligations, including contracts with Governments or with occupation or control authorities, whereby such authorities would continue, or undertake, in part or in whole, the care and maintenance of refugees and displaced persons in territories under their authority, under the supervision of the Organization;

(e) to conduct negotiations and conclude agreements with Governments;

(f) to consult and co-operate with public and private organizations whenever it is deemed advisable, in so far as such organizations share the purpose of the Organization -and observe the principles of the United Nations;

(g) to promote the conclusion of bilateral arrangements for- mutual assistance in the repatriation of displaced persons, having regard to the principles laid down in paragraph (c) (ii) of the resolution adopted by the General Assembly of the United Nations on 12 February 1946 regarding the problem of refugees (Annex III);

(h) to appoint staff, subject to the provisions of Article 9 of this Constitution;

(i) to undertake any project appropriate to the accomplishment of tile purposes of this Organization;

(j) to conclude agreements with countries able and willing to receive refugees and displaced persona for tile purpose of ensuring the protection of their legitimate rights and interests in so far as this may be necessary, and

(k) in general, to perform any other legal act appropriate to its purposes,

Article 3

Relationship to the United Nations

The relationship between the Organisation and the United Nations shall be established in an agreement between the

Organisation and the United Nations as provided in Articles 57 and 63 of the Charter of the United Nations,

Article 4

Membership

1. Membership in the Organisation is open to Members of the United Nations, Membership is also open to any other peace-loving States, not members of the United Nations, upon recommendation of the Executive Committee, by a two-thirds majority vote of members of the General Council present and voting, subject to the conditions of the agreement between the Organisation and the United Nations approved pursuant to article 3 of this Constitution.
2. Subject to the provisions of paragraph I of this article, the members of the Organization shall be those States whose duly authorized representatives sign this Constitution without reservation as to subsequent acceptance, and those States, which deposit with the Secretary-General of the United Nations their instruments of acceptance after their duly authorised representatives have signed this Constitution with such reservation.
3. Subject to the provisions of paragraph 1 of this article, those States, whose representatives have not signed the Constitution referred to in the previous paragraph, or which, having signed it, have not deposited the relevant instrument of acceptance within the following six months, may, however, be admitted as members of the Organization in the following cases:
   (a) if they undertake to liquidate any outstanding contributions in accordance with the relevant scale; or

(b) if they submit to the Organization a plan for the admission to their territory, as immigrants, refugees or displaced persons in such numbers, and on such settlement conditions as shall, in the opinion of the Organization, require from the applicant State an expenditure or investment equivalent, or approximately equivalent, to the contribution that they would be called upon, in accordance with tile relevant scale, to make to the budget of the Organization.

4. Those States which, on signing the Constitution, express their intention to avail themselves of clause (b) of paragraph 3 of this article may submit the plan referred to in that paragraph within the following three months, without prejudice to the presentation within six months of the relevant instrument of acceptance.

5. Members of the Organization which are suspended from the exercise of the rights and privileges of Membership of the United Nations shall, upon request of the latter, be suspended from the rights and privileges of this Organization.

6. Members of the Organization which are expelled from the United Nations shall automatically cease to be members of this Organization.

7. With the approval of the General Assembly of the United Nations, members of the Organization which are not members of the United Nations, and which have persistently violated the principles of the Charter of the United Nations may be suspended from the rights and privileges of the Organization, or expelled from its membership by the General Council,

8. A member of the Organization which has persistently

violated the principles contained in the present Constitution may be suspended from the rights and privileges of the Organization by the General Council, and with the approval of the General Assembly of the United Nations, may be expelled from the Organization.

9. A member of the Organization undertakes to afford its general support to the work of the Organization.
10. Any member may at any time give written notice of withdrawal to the Chairman of the Executive Committee, Such notice shall take effect one year after the date of its receipt by the Chairman of the Executive Committee.

Article 5

Organs

There are established as the principal organs of the Organization: a General Council, an Executive Committee land a Secretariat,

Article 6

The General Council

1. The ultimate policy-making body of the Organization shall be the General Council in which each member shall have one representative and such alternates and advisers as may be necessary. Each member shall have one vote in the General Council.
2. The General Council shall be convened in regular session not less than once a year by the Executive Committee provided, however, that for three years after the Organization comes into being the General Council shall be convened in regular session not less than twice a year. It may be convened in special

session whenever the Executive Committee shall deem necessary; and it shall be convened in special session by the Director-General within thirty days after a request for such a special session is received by the Director-General from one third of the members of the Council.

3. At the opening meeting of each session of the Genera! Council, the Chairman of the Executive Committee shall preside until the General Council has elected one of its members as Chairman for the session,

4. The General Council shall thereupon proceed to elect from among its members a first Vice-Chairman and a second Vice-Chairman, and Such other officers as it may deem necessary.

Article 7

Executive Committee

1. The Executive Committee shall perform such functions as may be necessary to give effect to the policies of the General Council, and may make, between sessions of the General Council, policy decisions of an emergency nature which it shall pass on to the Director-General, who shall be guided thereby, and shall report to the Executive Committee on the action which he has taken thereon. These decisions shall be subject to reconsideration by the General Council.

2. The Executive Committee of the General Council shall consist of the representatives of nine members of the Organization, Each member of the Executive Committee shall be elected for a two-year term by the General Council at a regular session of the Council. A member may continue to hold office on the Executive Committee during any such period as

may intervene between the conclusion of its term of office and the first succeeding meeting of the General Council at which an election takes place. A member shall be at all times eligible for re-election to the Executive Committee. If a vacancy occurs in the membership of the Executive Committee between two sessions of the General Council, the Executive Committee may fill the vacancy by itself appointing another member to hold office until the next meeting of the Council.

3. The Executive Committee shall elect a Chairman and a Vice-Chairman from among its members, the terms of office to be determined by the General Council.
4. Meetings of the Executive Committee shall be convened:

   (a) at the call of the Chairman, normally twice a month;

   (b) whenever any representative of a member of the Executive Committee shall request the convening of a meeting, by a letter addressed to the Director-General, in which case the meeting-shall be convened within seven days of the date of the receipt of the request;

   (c) in the case of a vacancy occurring in the Chairmanship, the Director-General shall convene a meeting at which the first item on the agenda shall be the election of a Chairman,
5. The Executive Committee may, in order to investigate the situation in the field, either as a body or through a delegation of its members, visit camps, hostels or assembly points within the control of the Organization, and may give instructions to the

Director-General in consequence of the reports of such visits.

6. The Executive Committee shall receive the reports of the Director-General as provided in paragraph 6 of article 8 of this Constitution, and, after consideration thereof, shall request the Director- General to transmit these reports to the Central Council with such comments as the Executive Committee may consider appropriate. These reports and such comments shall be transmitted to all members of the General Council before its next regular session and shall be published. The Executive Committee may request the Director-General to submit such further reports as may be deemed necessary.

Article 8

Administration

1. The chief administrative officer of the Organization shall be the Director-General. He shall be responsible to the General Council and the Executive Committee and shall carry out the administrative and executive functions of the Organization in accordance with the decisions of the General Council and the Executive Committee, and shall report on the action taken thereon,
2. The Director-General shall be nominated by the Executive Committee and appointed by the General Council. If no person acceptable to the General Council is nominated by the Executive Committee, the General Council may proceed to appoint a person who has not been nominated by Committee, When a vacancy occurs in the office of the Director-General, the Executive Committee may appoint an Acting Director-

General to assume all the duties and functions of the office until a Director-General can be appointed by the General Council,

3. The Director-General shall serve under a contract which shall be signed on behalf of the Organisation by the Chairman of the Executive Committee and it shall be a clause of such contract that six months' notice of termination can be given on either side, In exceptional circumstances, the Executive Committee, subject to subsequent confirmation by the General Council, has the power to relieve the Director-General of his duties by a two-thirds majority vote of the members if, in the Committee's opinion, his conduct is such as to warrant such action,
4. The staff of the Organisation shall be appointed by the Director-General under regulations to be established by the General Council.
5. The Director-General shall be present, or be represented by one of his subordinate officers, at all meetings of the General Council, or the Executive Committee and of all other committees and sub-committees. He or his representatives may participate in any such meeting but shall have no vote.
   (a) The Director-General shall prepare at the end of each half-year period a report on the work of the Organization. The report prepared at the end of each alternate period of six months shall relate to the work of the Organization during the preceding year and shall give a full account of the activities of the Organization during that period. These reports shall be submitted to the Executive Committee for consideration, and thereafter shall be transmitted to the General

Council together with any comments of the Executive Committee thereon, as provided by paragraph 6 of article 7 of this Constitution.

(b) At every special session of the General Council the Director-General shall present a statement of the work of the Organization since the last meeting.

Article 9

Staff

1. The paramount consideration in the employment of the staff and in the determination of the conditions of service shall be the necessity of securing the highest standards of efficiency, competence and integrity. A further consideration in the employment of the staff shall be adherence to the principles laid down in the present Constitution. Due regard shall be paid to the importance of recruiting staff on an appropriate geographical basis, and of employing an adequate number of persons from the countries of origin of the displaced persons.
2. No person shall be employed by the Organization who is excluded under Part II, other than paragraph 5, of Annex I to this Constitution, from becoming the concern of the Organization.
3. In the performance of their duties, the Director-General and the staff shall not seek or receive instructions from any Government or from any other authority external to the Organization. They shall refrain from any action which might reflect on their position as international officials responsible only to the Organization. Each member of the Organization undertakes to respect the exclusively

international character of the responsibilities of the Director-General and the staff and not to seek to influence them in the discharge of their responsibilities.

Article 10

Finance

1. The Director-General shall submit, through the Executive Committee, to the General Council an annual budget, covering the necessary administrative, operational and large-scale re-settlement expenditures of the Organization, and from time to time such supplementary budgets as may be required. The Executive Committee shall transmit the budget to the General Council with any remarks it may deem appropriate. Upon final approval of a budget by the General Council, the total under each of these three headings to wit, "administrative", "operational" and "large-scale re-settlement"-shall be allocated to the members in proportions for each heading to be determined from time to time by a two-thirds majority vote of the members of the General Council present and voting.
2. Contributions shall be payable, as a result of negotiations undertaken at the request of members between the Organization and such members, in kind or in such currency as may be provided for in a decision by the General Council, having regard to currencies in which the anticipated expenditure of the Organization will be effected from time to time, regardless of the currency in which the budget is expressed.
3. Each member undertakes to contribute to the

Organization its share of the administrative expenses as determined and allocated under paragraphs I and 2 of this article.

4. Each member shall contribute to the operational expenditures— except for large-scale re-settlement expenditures-as determined and allocated under paragraphs I and 2 of this article, subject to the requirements of the constitutional procedure of such members. The members undertake to contribute to the large-scale re-settlement expenditures on a voluntary basis and subject to the requirements of their constitutional procedure.
5. A member of the Organization, which, after the expiration of a period of three months following the date of the coming into force of this Constitution, has not paid its financial contribution to the Organization for the first financial year, shall have no vote in the General Council or the Executive Committee until Such contribution has been paid.
6. Subject to the provisions of paragraph 5 of this article, a member of the Organization which is 'in arrears in the payment of its financial contributions to the Organization shall have no vote in the General Council or the Executive Committee if the amount of its arrears equals or exceeds the amount of the contributions due from it for the preceding one full year.
7. The General Council may, nevertheless, permit such members to vote if it is satisfied that the failure to pay is due to conditions, beyond the control of such members.
8. The administrative budget of the Organization shall be submitted annually to the General Assembly Of

the United Nations for such review and recommendation as the General Assembly may deem appropriate. The agreement under which the Organization shall be brought into relationship with the United Nations under article 3 of this Constitution may provide, inter alia, for the approval of the administrative budget of the Organization by the General Assembly of the United Nations.

9. Without prejudice to the provisions concerning supplementary budgets in paragraph I of this article, the following exceptional arrangements shall apply in respect of the financial year in which this Constitution comes into force:
   (a) the budget shall be the provisional budget set forth in Annex 11 to this Constitution; and
   (b) the amounts to be contributed by the members shall be in the proportions set forth in Annex II to this Constitution.

Article 11

Headquarters and Other Offices

1. The Organization shall establish its headquarters at Paris or at Geneva, as the General Council shall decide, and all meetings of the General Council and the Executive Committee shall be held at this headquarters, unless a majority of the members of the General Council or the Executive Committee have agreed, at a previous meeting or by correspondence with the Director-General, to meet elsewhere.
2. The Executive Committee may establish such regional and other offices and representations as may be necessary.

3. All offices and representations shall be established only with the consent of the Government in authority in the place of establishment.

Article 12

Procedure

1. The General Council shall adopt its own rules of procedure, following in general the rules of procedure of the Economic and Social Council of the United Nations, wherever appropriate, and with such modifications as the General Council shall deem desirable. The Executive Committee shall regulate its own procedure subject to any decisions of the General Council in respect thereto.
2. Unless otherwise provided in the Constitution or by action of the General Council, motions shall be carried by simple majority of the members present and voting in the General Council and the Executive Committee.

Article 13

Status, Immunities and Privileges

1. The Organization shall enjoy in the territory of each of its members such legal capacity as may be necessary for the exercise of its functions and the fulfillment of its objectives.
2. (a) The Organization shall enjoy in the territory of each of its members such privileges and immunities as may be necessary for the exercise of its functions and the fulfilment of its objectives.

   (b) Representatives of members, officials and administrative personnel of the Organization shall similarly enjoy such privileges and immunities as are necessary for the independent exercise of their functions in connection with the Organization.

3. Such legal status, privileges and immunities shall be defined in an agreement to be prepared by the Organization after consultation with the Secretary-General of the United Nations. The agreement shall be open to accession by all members and shall continue in force as between the Organization and every member which accedes to the agreement.

Article 14

Relations with Other Organizations

1. Subject to the provisions of the agreement to be negotiated with the United Nations, pursuant to article 3 of this Constitution, the Organization may establish such effective relationships as may be desirable with other international organizations.
2. The Organization may assume all or part of the functions, and acquire all or part of the resources, assets and liabilities of any inter-governmental organization or agency, the purposes and functions of which lie within the scope of the Organization. Such action may be taken either through mutually acceptable arrangements with the competent authorities of such organizations or agencies, or pursuant to authority conferred upon the Organization by international convention or agreement.

Article 15

Relationship with Authorities of Countries of Location of Refugees and Displaced Persons

The relationship of the Organization with the

Governments or administrations of countries in which displaced persons or refugees are located, and the conditions under which it will operate in such countries, shall be determined by agreements to be negotiated by it with such Governments or administrations in accordance with the terms of this Constitution.

Article 16

Amendment of Constitution

Texts of proposed amendments to this Constitution shall be communicated by the Director-General to members at least three months in advance of their consideration by the General Council. Amendments shall come into effect when adopted by a two-thirds majority of the members of the General Council present and voting and accepted by two-thirds of the members in accordance with their respective constitutional processes, provided, however, that amendments involving new obligations for members shall come into force in respect of each member only on acceptance by it.

Article 17

Interpretation

1. The Chinese, English, French, Russian and Spanish texts of this Constitution shall be regarded as equally authentic.
2. Subject to Article 96 of the Charter of the United Nations and of Chapter 11 of the Statute of the International Court of Justice, any question or dispute concerning the interpretation or application of this Constitution shall be referred to the International Court of Justice, unless the General Council or the parties to such dispute agree to another mode of settlement,

Article 18
Entry into Force

1. (a) States may become parties to this Constitution by;
   - (i) signature without reservation as to approval,
   - (ii) signature subject to approval followed by acceptance;
   - (iii) acceptance,

   (b) acceptance shall be effected by the deposit of a formal instrument with the Secretary-General of the United Nations.
2. This Constitution shall come into force when at least fifteen States, whose required contributions to Part I of the operational budget as set forth in Annex 11 of this Constitution amount to not less than seventy-five per cent of the total thereof, have become parties to it.
3. In accordance with Article 102 of the Charter of the United Nations, the Secretary-General of the United Nations will register this Constitution, when it has been signed, without reservation as to approval, on behalf of one State or upon deposit of the first instrument of acceptance.
4. The Secretary-General of the United Nations will inform States parties to this Constitution of the date when it has come into force: he will also inform them of the dates when other States have become parties to this Constitution,

In Faith Whereof the undersigned, duly authorized for that purpose, have signed this Constitution.

Done at Flushing Meadow, New York, this fifteenth day of December, one thousand nine hundred and forty-six, in a single copy in the Chinese, English, French, Russian and Spanish languages. The original texts shall be deposited in the archives of the. United Nations. The Secretary-General of the United Nations will send certified copies of the texts to each of the signatory Governments and, upon the coming into force of the Constitution and the election of a Director-General to the Director-General of the Organisation.

9

Convention on the Reduction of Statelessness

"Without the help of others, any one of us would die, naked and starved. Consider the bread upon our tables, the clothes upon our backs, the luxuries that make life pleasant; hew many men worked in sunlit fields, in dark mines, in the fierce heat of modern metal, and among the looms and wheels of countless factories, in order to create them for our use and enjoyment."

—*Alfred E. Smith*

The Contracting States

Acting in pursuance of resolution 896 (DC), adopted by the General Assembly of the United Nations on 4 December 1954.

Considering it desirable to reduce Statelessness by international agreement,

Have agreed as follows:

Article 1

1. A Contracting State shall grant its nationality to a person born in its territory who would otherwise be stateless. Such nationality shall be

(a) at birth, by operation of law, or

(b) upon an application being lodged with the appropriate authority, by or on behalf of the person concerned, in the manner prescribed by the national law. Subject to the provisions of paragraph 2 of this Article, no such application may be rejected.

A Contracting State which provides for the grant of its nationality in accordance with sub-paragraph (b) of this paragraph may also provide for the grant of its nationality by operation of law at such age and subject to such conditions as may be prescribed by the national law.

2. A Contracting State may make the grant of its nationality in accordance with sub-paragraph (b) of paragraph I of this Article subject to one or more of the following conditions:

(a) that the application is lodged during a period, fixed by the Contracting State, beginning not later than at the age of eighteen years and ending not earlier than at the age of twenty-one years, so, however, that the person concerned shall be allowed at least one year during which he may himself make the application without having to obtain legal authorization to do so;

(b) that the person concerned has habitually resided in the territory of the Contracting State for such period as may be fixed by that State, not exceeding five years immediately preceding the lodging of the application nor ten years in all,

(c) that the person concerned has neither been convicted of an offence against national security nor has been sentenced to imprisonment for a term of five years or more on a criminal charge;

(d) that the person concerned has always been stateless.

3. Notwithstanding the provisions of paragraphs I (b) and 2 of this Article, a child born in wedlock in the territory of a Contracting State, whose mother has the nationality of that State, shall acquire, at birth that nationality if it otherwise would be stateless.
4. A Contracting State shall grant its nationality to i person who would otherwise be stateless and who is unable to acquire the nationality of the Contracting State in whose territory he was born because he has passed the age for lodging his application or has not fulfilled the required residence conditions, if the nationality of one of his parents- at the time of the, person's birth was that of the Contracting State first above mentioned. If his parents did not possess the same nationality at the time of his birth, the question whether the nationality of the person concerned should follow that, of the father or that of tile mother shall be determined by the national law of such Contracting State. If application for such nationality is required, the application shall be made to the appropriate authority by or on behalf of the applicant in the manner prescribed by the national law. Subject to the provisions of paragraph 5 of this Article, such application shall not be refused.
5. The Contracting State may make the grant of its nationality in accordance with the provisions of paragraph 4 of this Article subject to one or more of the following conditions:

(a) that the application is lodged before the applicant reaches an age, being not less than twenty-three years, fixed by the Contracting State;

(b) that the person concerned has habitually resided in the territory of the Contracting State for such period immediately preceding the lodging of the application, not exceeding three years, as may be fixed by that State:

(c) that the person concerned has always been stateless,

Article 2

A foundling found in the territory of a Contracting State shall, in the absence of proof to the contrary, be considered to have been born within that territory of parents possessing the nationality of that State.

Article 3

For the purpose of determining the obligations of Contracting States under this Convention, birth oil a ship or in all aircraft shall be deemed to have taken place in the territory of tile State whose flag the ship files or in the territories of the States in which the aircraft is registered as the case may be

Article 4

1. A Contracting State shall grant its nationality to a person, not born in the territory of a Contracting State, who would otherwise be stateless, if the nationality of one of his parents at the time of the person's birth was that of that State, If his parents did not possess the same nationality at the time of his birth, the question whether the nationality of

the person concerned should follow that of the father or that of the mother shall be determined by the national law of such Contracting State, Nationality granted in accordance with the provisions of this paragraph shall be granted-

(a) at birth, by operation of law, or

(b) upon an application being lodged with the appropriate authority} by or on behalf of the person concerned, in the manner prescribed by the national law Subject to the provisions of paragraph 2 of this Article, no such application may be rejected,

2. A Contracting State may make the grant of its nationality in accordance with the provisions of paragraph I of this Article subject to one or more of the following conditions:

(a) that the application is lodged before the applicant reaches an age, being not less than twenty-three years, fixed by the Contracting State;

(b) that the person concerned has habitually resided in the territory of the Contracting State for such period immediately preceding the lodging of the application, not exceeding three years, as may be fixed by that State;

(c) that the person concerned has not been convicted of an offence against national security;

(d) that the person concerned has always been stateless.

Article 5

1. If the law of a Contracting State entails loss of nationality as a consequence of any change in the

personal status of a person such as marriage, termination of marriage, legitimation, recognition or adoption, such loss shall be conditional upon possession or acquisition of another nationality,

2. If, under the law of a Contracting State, a child born out of wedlock loses the nationality of that State in consequence of a recognition of affiliation, he shall be given an opportunity to recover that nationality by written application to the appropriate authority, and the conditions governing Such application shall not be more rigorous than those laid down in paragraph 2 of Article 1 of this Convention.

If the law of a Contracting State provides for loss of its nationality by a person's spouse or children as a consequence of that person losing or being deprived of that nationality, such loss shall be conditional upon their possession or acquisition of another nationality. Article 7

1. (a) If the law of a Contracting State permits renunciation of nationality, such renunciation shall not result in loss of nationality unless the person concerned, possesses or acquired another nationality,

   (b) The provisions of sub-paragraph (a) of this paragraph shall not apply where their application would be inconsistent with the principles stated in Articles 13 and 14 of the Universal Declaration of Human Rights approved on 10 December 1948 by the General Assembly of the United Nations.

2. A national of a Contracting State who seeks naturalization in a foreign country shall not lose his nationality unless he acquired or has been accorded

assurance of acquiring the nationality of that foreign country.

3. Subject to the provisions of paragraphs 4 and 5 of this Article, a national of a Contracting State shall not lose, his nationality, so a$ to become stateless, on the ground of departure, residence abroad, failure to register or on any similar ground.
4. A naturalized person may lose his nationality on account of residence abroad for a period, not less than seven consecutive years, specified by the law of the Contracting State concerned if he fails to declare to the appropriate authority his intention to retain his nationality.
5. In the case of a national of a Contracting State, born outside its territory, the law of that State may make the retention of its nationality after the expiry of one year from his attaining his majority conditional upon residence at that time in the territory of the State or registration with the appropriate authority.
6. Except in the circumstances mentioned in this Article, a person shall not lose the nationality of a Contracting State, if such loss would render him stateless, notwithstanding that such loss is not expressly prohibited by any other provisions of this Convention.

Article 8

1. A Contracting State shall not deprive a person of his nationality if such deprivation would fender him stateless.
2. Not withstanding the provisions of paragraph I of this Article, a person may be deprived of the nationality of a Contracting State:

(a) in the circumstances in which, under paragraphs 4 and 5 of Article 7, it is permissible that a person should lose his nationality,

(b) where the nationality has been obtained by misrepresentation or fraud,

3. Notwithstanding the provisions of paragraph of this Article, a Contracting State may retain the right to deprive a person of his nationality, if at the time of signature, ratification or accession it specifies its retention of such right on one or more of the following grounds, being grounds existing in its national law at that time:

   (a) that, inconsistently with his duty of loyalty to the Contracting State, the person

      (i) has, in disregard of an express prohibition by the Contracting State rendered or continued to render service to, or received or continued to receive emoluments from another State, or

      (ii) has conducted himself in a manner seriously prejudicial to the vital interests of the State;

   (b) that the person has taken an oath, or made a formal declaration, of allegiance to another State, or given definite evidence of his determination to repudiate his allegiance to the Contracting State.

4. A Contracting State shall not exercise a power of deprivation permitted by paragraphs 2 or 3 of this Article except in accordance with law, which shall provide for the person concerned the right to a fair hearing *by* a court or other independent body.

Article 9

A Contracting State may not deprive any person or group of persons of their nationality on racial, ethnic, religious or political grounds.

Article 10

1. Every treaty between Contracting Stales providing for the transfer of territory shall include provisions designed to secure that no person shall become stateless as a result of the transfer. A Contracting State shall use its best endeavours to secure that any such treaty made by it with a. State which is not a party to this Convention include~ such provisions,
2. In the absence of such, provisions a Contracting' State tc which territory is transferred or which otherwise acquires territory shall confer its nationality on such, persons as would otherwise become stateless as a result of the transfer or acquisition.

Article 11

The Contracting States shall promote the establishment within the framework of the United Nations, as soon as may be after the deposit of the sixth instrument of ratification or accession, of a body to which a person claiming the benefit of this Convention may apply for the examination of his claim and for assistance in presenting it to the appropriate authority.

Article 12

1. In relation to a Contracting State which does not, in accordance with the provisions of paragraph I of Article I or of Article 4 of this Convention, grant its nationality at birth by operation of law, the, provisions of paragraph I of Article I or of Article 4, as the case

may be, shall apply to persons born before as well as to persons born after the entry into force of this Convention.

2. The provisions of paragraph 4 of Article 1 of the Convention shall apply to persons born before as well as to persons born after its entry into force.
3. The provisions of Article 2 of this Convention shall apply only to foundlings found in the territory of a Contracting State after the entry into force of the Convention foe that State.

Article 13

This Convention shall not be construed as affecting any provisions there conducive to the reduction of statelessness which may be contained in the law of any Contracting State now or hereafter in force, or may be contained in any other convention, treaty or agreement now or hereafter in force between two or more Contracting States.

Article 14

Any dispute between Contracting States concerning the interpretation or application of this Convention which cannot be settled by other means shall be Submitted to the International Court of Justice at the request of any one of the parties to the dispute.

Article 15

1. This Convention shall apply to all non-self-governing, trust, colonial and other non-metropolitan territories for the international relations of which any Contracting State is responsible: the Contracting State concerned shall, subject to the provisions of paragraph 2 of this Article, at the time of signature, ratification or accession, declare the non-metropolitan

territory or territories to which the Convention shall apply ipso facto as a result of such signature, ratification or accession.

2. In any case in which, for the purpose of nationality, a non-metropolitan territory is not treated as one with the metropolitan territory, or in any case in which the previous consent of a non-metropolitan territory is required by the constitutional laws or practices of the Contracting State or of the non-metropolitan territory for the application of the Convention to that territory, that Contracting State shall endeavour to secure the needed consent of the non-metropolitan territory within the period of twelve months from the date of signature of the Convention by that Contracting State, and when Such consent has been obtained the Contracting State shall notify the Secretary-General of the United Nations. This Convention shall apply to the territory or territories named in such notification from the date of its receipt by the Secretary-General.
3. After the expiry of the twelve-month period mentioned in paragraph 2 of this article, the Contracting States concerned shall inform the Secretary-General of the results of the consultations with those non-metropolitan territories for whose international relations they are responsible and whose consent to the application of this Convention may have been withheld.

Article 16

1. This Convention shall be open for signature at the Headquarters of the United Nations from 30 August 1961 to 31 May 1962.

2. This Convention shall be open for signature on behalf of:
   (a) any State Member of the United Nations;
   (b) any other State invited to attend the United Nations Conference on the Elimination or Reduction of Future Statelessness;
   (c) any State to which an invitation to sign or to accede may be addressed *by* the General Assembly of the United Nations.
3. This Convention shall be ratified and the instruments of ratification shall be deposited with the Secretary-General of the United Nations.
4. This Convention shall be open for accession by the States referred to in paragraph 2 of this Article. Accession shall be effected by the deposit of an instrument of accession with the Secretary-General of the United Nations.

Article 17

1. At the time of signature, ratification or accession any State may make a reservation in respect of Articles 11,14 or 15.
2. No other reservations to this Convention shall be admissible.

Article 18

1. This Convention shall enter into force two years after the date of the deposit of the sixth instrument of ratification or accession.
2. For each State ratifying or acceding to this Convention after the deposit of the sixth instrument of ratification or accession, it shall enter into force on the ninetieth

day after the deposit by such State of its instrument of ratification or accession or on the date on which this Convention enters into force in accordance with the provisions of paragraph 1 of this Article, whichever is the later.

Article 19

1. Any Contracting State may denounce this Convention at any time by a written notification addressed to the Secretary-General of the United Nations. Such denunciation shall like effect for the Contracting State concerned one year after the date of its receipt by the Secretary-General.
2. In cases where, in accordance with the provisions of Article 15, this Convention has become applicable to a non-metropolitan territory of a Contracting State, that State may at any time thereafter, with the consent of the territory concerned, give notice to the Secretary -General of the United Nations denouncing this Convention separately in respect of that territory. The denunciation shall take effect one year after the date of the receipt of such notice by the Secretary-General who shall notify all other Contracting States of such notice and the date of receipt thereof.

Article 20

1. The Secretary-General of the United Nations shall notify all Members of the United Nations and the non-member States referred to in Article 16 of the following particulars:

   (a) signatures, ratifications and accessions, under Article 16;

   (b) reservations under Article 17;

(c) the date upon which this Convention enters into force in pursuance of Article 18;

(d) denunciations under Article 19.

2. The Secretary-General of the United Nations shall, after the deposit of the sixth instrument of ratification or accession at the latest, bring to the attention of the General Assembly the question of the establishment, in accordance with Article 11, of such a body as therein mentioned.:

Article 21

This Convention shall be registered by the Secretary-General of the United Nations on the date of its entry into force.

In witness whereof the undersigned Plenipotentiaries have signed this Convention.

Done at New York, this thirtieth day of August, one thousand nine hundred and sixty-one, in a single copy, of which the Chinese, English, French, Russian and Spanish texts are equally authentic and which shall be deposited in the archives of the United Nations, and certified copies of which shall be delivered by the Secretary-General of the United Nations to all Members of the United Nations and to the non-member States referred.

10

CASE STUDIES

"Most people fancy themselves innocent of those crimes of which they cannot be convicted."

—*Seneca*

Southern Africa's Uprooted : A Case Study

Suffering and terror are the daily bread of the Mozambican and Angolan people. As conflict continues to ravage their countries, some are starving and many are being killed, often for no other reason than someone with a gun decided to shoot them. Others are maimed, their ears cut off, or their legs blown off by landmines. In Mozambique, children are abducted and forced to work for their captors. Worse yet, they are used as instruments of terror, forced to shoot and kill, or be shot and killed. Throughout the region, millions of people have fled their homes to escape the violence around them. Most are languishing in refugee camps, unable to grow their own food, dependent on aid that, increasingly, is not forthcoming. -Yet, in the midst of so much suffering, there is also hope. In both Mozambique and Angola, government and rebel negotiators have taken a few tentative steps on the long and arduous road towards peace. Although there have been setbacks, particularly in Angola, there is pressure on all parties-both from neighboring countries and the rest of the international community-for resolutions to the conflicts that have devastated the two countries and sent refugees fleeing throughout the region. For many refugees, the negotiations have kindled hope. Hope for peace, for security, and for a return home. But if the current initiatives fail, there will be grave consequences. For the people of Mozambique and Angola, the terror will continue. Refugees may find host countries unwilling to extend their hospitality.

Death, Destruction, and Displacement

In Mozambique, fighting continues even though the government and the Mozambican National Resistance (RENAMO) are moving tentatively towards peace talks. More than 100,000 Mozambicans have been purposely killed, and almost 500,000 children are said to have died as a result of the conflict; countless other children have been orphaned, separated from their families, or kidnapped by RENAMO, a group that some have labeled the Khmer Rouge of Africa. An estimated 1, 7 million Mozambicans are internally displaced; another 2.9 million who have been able to remain in their homes are affected by the conflict, unable to grow their crops because of the lack of security and partly or wholly dependent on food aid. One and a quarter million Mozambicans have fled to neighboring countries; every month, another 13,000 arrive in Malawi alone, Many of the country's schools, hospitals, and other public buildings have been destroyed. Transportation is difficult to impossible in many parts of the country because of RENAMO attacks and the destruction of trucks, roads, and bridges. The conflict in Angola, between the government and rebels from the National Union for the Total Independence of Angola (UNITA), also continues to ravage the country. Reliable estimates of how many Angolans have been killed do not exist, but the high numbers of people, that have been maimed, and of children reported to have died in the conflict, suggest that the death toll in Angola is also very high. According to government estimates, 638,000 Angolans are internally displaced; hundred of thousands more-many of them people also displaced by the fighting-are, living in Urban centers in destitute conditions. More than 438,000 Angolan refugees have sought refuge in neighboring countries. The first fled to those countries to escape fighting between liberation groups and the Portuguese colonial administration. Most, however, fled more recently, escaping the conflict between the government and UNITA. In the countries of asylum, Mozambican and Angolan refugees have met quite different receptions. In Zambia and Zaire, the governments have by and large given their land on which to grow their own food, and many are self-sufficient.

In Zimbabwe, where land and security are politically sensitive issues, many of the refugees are living in crowded, fenced-in refugee camps, and forced repatriation of refugees to Mozambique continues. Malawi has done its best to welcome the refugees, but the scale of the influx-in some areas refugees outnumber Malawians by three to two-represents an overwhelming burden for that tiny, already crowded country. Refugees who fled to South Africa are in the most precarious situation. The United Nations High Commissioner for Refugees (UNHCR), the agency mandated by the international community to protect and assist refugees, is barred from South Africa, and refugees there live in constant fear of deportation. Mozambicans and Angolans are by no means the only refugee groups in southern Africa. South African refugees, although small in numbers compared to Mozambicans and Angolans, face particular difficulties. All the governments in the region voice strong support for majority rule in South Africa, and many of them host at least small numbers of South African refugees. Count-ties bordering South Africa fear, however, that too close an association with the refugees or with the African National Congress (ANC)-the South African group at the front line of the struggle for majority rule in that country-may lead to renewed military and economic retaliation by South Africa. Not all South African refugees feel welcomed in neighboring countries. One refugee who has been in Zimbabwe for many years says that "South Africans are discouraged from seeking asylum here. The government would like to keep the number of refugees at a minimum, and their political activity is limited."

Namibian refugees enjoyed a warmer reception while in asylum, but the majority have returned home now that Namibian independence is at hand (barring any catastrophic, last-minute complications). Their return, however, has not been totally smooth. Many have faced security problems, and, although millions of dollars have been spent to send them home, relatively little has been done to help them make a new start during their first months there. There are also approximately 12,000 Zairean refugees in Angola. A new repatriation program is underway, however, which is expected to return some 2,000 of them home. *A Dark Cloud* Today, a dark cloud hangs over refugees in southern Africa. UNHCR is facing a critical funding crisis. Major new refugee influxes and costly repatriations have drained its resources. The agency is almost entirely dependent on contributions from UN member nations for its operations. Although financial support from donor governments has generally increased in recent years, it has not kept up with the rising cost of caring for existing refugees, responding to new emergencies, and assisting refugees to go home when that is possible. U.S. support for UNHCR has fluctuated in recent years, though its contribution has decreased as a total percentage of the UNHCR budget. Because of the funding crisis, UNHCR has already cut services to refugees, asserting that these cuts have been in important but non-life-threatening areas such as education, legal aid, and programs to promote self-sufficiency. But ominous signs point to cuts in essential areas such as medical services and nutritional programs, and southern Africa could be one of the worst-hit regions. In Malawi, for example, UNHCR's cash-flow problems have already meant that contractors have not been paid, and according to UNHCR, "plans to replace highly inadequate medical facilities ... have had to be cancelled ... [and) nutritional standards are likely to decline as a result." If additional funds are not forthcoming, UNHCR adds, the organization "may not even cover survival needs."

This has grave implications for southern Africa. While most asylum countries now welcome or tolerate refugees, if they have to shoulder an even greater burden, that hospitality may diminish. It is not only UNHCR funding that is drying up however. This year, donor countries' humanitarian assistance to Mozambique-on which that country depends in order to feed its displaced and affected populations-has fallen well short of the need. According to the World Food Program (WFP), if more food aid is not forthcoming, there could be "a serious human tragedy." Food aid to Angola is also far below the need, and the consequences there could be equally grave.

In 1989, there have been breakthroughs in seemingly intractable conflicts. UN Security Council Resolution 435, which paves the way for Namibian independence, is being implemented. Namibian refugees have returned home, elections were held in November, and full independence is due in 1990. African heads of state, meeting in Zaire in June, apparently received Angolan government and UNITA assurances that they would begin peace talks. As of November 1989, however, the talks had not begun. The Mozambican government and RENAMO have had preliminary communications through mediators, and both parties have at least voiced a desire for peace, but have also not begun direct negotiations. The success or failure of these processes will have major consequences. Failure will mean continued terror for the people of Mozambique and Angola, Yet peace, though longed for, carries its own burden. Any sudden return of millions of refugees and displaced people to their home areas would severely strain either country's already stretched-resources. Without adequate planning and a quick, coordinated, international response, such a repatriation could create a staggering emergency.

Recent History

The history of southern Africa includes many examples of involuntary population movements. The slave trade, for centuries the scourge of southern Africans, forced countless numbers of people in what are now Angola and Mozambique to flee their homes to avoid capture; The staggering number of people "exported"' as slaves from Angola (four million) and Mozambique, (one million) bears witness to the vast scale of that heinous institution. During the first half of this century, harsh colonial policies and the search for work also forced hundreds of thousands of Mozambicans to migrate to South Africa and to what are now Malawi and Zimbabwe. In recent years, large numbers of people were displaced by fighting associated with struggles for independence and majority rule.

But the conflicts that have generated most of the refugee and displaced populations in southern Africa today are those between the post-independence governments in

Mozambique and Angola, and the insurgent groups operating in those countries, RENAMO and UNITA.

Mozambique: The FRELIMO Government and RENAMO Mozambican exiles from various countries, meeting in Tanzania in 1962, established the Front for the Liberation of Mozambique (FRELIMO), which gained recognition from the Organization of African Unity (OAU) as the legitimate representative of the Mozambican people. Although FRELIMO was plagued by ideological and ethnic disputes during its early years, militarily it scored victories that enabled it to gain effective control of the northern third of Mozambique. In 1974, a coup by military reformists in Portugal led to an offer of independence for Mozambique. Despite FRELIMO's lack of political organization in most of the country, in 1975 the Portuguese (eager to end their involvement in Mozambique) transferred all governmental authority directly to FRELIMO, which formed a one-party, socialist government. The vast, majority of Portuguese quickly fled.

Many of the new government's policies ultimately proved to be unpopular and economically disastrous. In the early 1980s, however, recognizing these failings, the government instituted reforms in the economy and moved forcefully to improve relations with the West. Although the West welcomed Mozambique's reforms, and ties have improved (the United States, Italy, and Britain now give Mozambique considerable assistance), throughout the 1980s Mozambique has been embroiled in a devastating conflict that has played havoc with efforts to revive its economy. At the root of that conflict are the violence and terrorism perpetrated by RENAMO. RENAMO was created by Ian Smith's white minority government in Southern Rhodesia (now Zimbabwe) to stir opposition to the FRELIMO government. After Zimbabwe attained majority rule in 1980, South Africa became

RENAMO's main source of support, providing that country a vehicle for its policy of destabilization in the region. The U.S. Committee for Refugees (USCR) was among the first to raise the alarm on the human tragedy in Mozambique. In November 1986, USCR published an issue paper, Shattered Land, Fragile Asylum, which warned that "RENAMO's wanton slaying and brutalization of the civilian population" was forcing hundreds of thousands of Mozarribicans to flee the country. In April 1988, the U.S. State Department issued a pivotal report that documented RENAMO's pervasive pattern of atrocities against civilians.

According to refugees interviewed. RENAMO extracts labor and food from civilians, for whom the only reciprocity, according to the report, "is the possibility of staying alive." The report says that, although government soldiers are not without blame, refugees interviewed implicated RENAMO soldiers in about 94 percent of the killings and atrocities inflicted upon them and their neighbors, causing them to flee. The South African government claims that it no longer supports RENAMO, but most observers believe that at least some elements within the South African government-as well as other private sources in South Africa—continue to provide material, logistic, and technical support to RENAMO.

Angola: The MPLA Government and UNITA In 1956, a number of small political associations opposed to the repressive Portuguese colonial administration in Angola formed the Popular Movement, for the Liberation of Angola (MPLA). In 1961, the MPLA and another, smaller liberation group were involved in incidents that triggered a popular uprising against Portuguese rule. Portugal's response to the uprising was brutal. Its saturation bombing of villages and its use of napalm forced more than 60,000 Angolans to seek refuge in Zaire, while the death toll within Angola was estimated at

50,000. In 1966. Jonas Savimbi, an Ovirnbundu (the largest and most widely dispersed ethnic group in Angola) who had been associated with yet another liberation group, the National Front for the Liberation of Angola (FNLA), established UNITA. All three-MPLA, FNLA, and UNITA-fought guerrilla wars against the Portuguese between the late 1960s and April 1974, when the coup in Portugal suddenly and unexpectedly ended the fighting. By then, more than 100,000 Angolans had died and another 500.000 had been forced into exile. Despite conflicts among the three liberation movements, in January 1975 they agreed to a common front in negotiating for independence from Portugal. Within weeks, however", the three movements' political confrontation gave way to military conflict, and to an unprecedented level of violence. Foreign powers began to support each of the three movements: the United States and China provided funding to the FNLA; the Soviet Union and Cuba came to the aid of the MPLA, both financially and militarily; and South Africa intervened on the side of UNITA. South Africa's involvement with UNITA provided Pretoria a useful too] for destabilizing Angola. On November 11,1975, as scheduled, Angola officially became independent.

In the absence of a single entity to assume the powers of government, Portugal abdicated, handed over authority to "the people of Angola," and left. MPLAs control of the capital allowed it to take over the reins of government. More than 300,000 Portuguese left Angola during the period preceding and following independence. The social MPLA government and UNITA, which identifies itself as pro-Western, have baffled ever since. The conflict, combined with misguided government policies, bureaucratic inefficiencies, and natural disasters, has resulted in drastic declines in agricultural production. Consequently, Angola has faced severe food shortages.

The government has recently modified some of its more unsuccessful and unpopular agricultural policies and established a more mixed economy of public and private sectors, but, while it has reached out to the West, it has been unsuccessful in its bid to improve relations with the United States, which has been providing "covert" military aid to UNITA since 1986.

11

Temporary Protection, Repatriation Aid and Development

"Don't be afraid of criticism. Anyone who can fill out a laundry slip thinks of himself as a writer. Anyone who can't fill out a laundry slip thinks of himself as a critic."

—*Georte Seation*

The literature on refugee aid and development has long recognized that attention must be paid both to the countries of asylum and of return. Chief among the principles is that emergency and care and maintenance assistance, as well as more development-oriented aid, should be targeted in such a way that local hosts receive benefits, not merely the refugees or returnees. This approach preserves the generous attitudes of host country populations toward refugees and of stayee populations toward returnees. The literature also emphasizes that the developmental implications of emergency assistance should be taken into account at the outset, and that the local population and the refugees or returnees should, in principle, be incorporated into the planning and implementation of projects. Other widely recognized principles call for the linkage of infrastructural (bricks and mortar type projects) with self-reliance and income generation components (the human improvement aspect of development).

There is a widespread assumption that dispensers of refugee aid should be conscious of its developmental effects, and that development aid should account for the impact that refugees and returnees have on the economic and social infrastructure and population of refugee and returnee-affected regions. There is less agreement about how such principles ought to be effected and by whom, and there are ongoing experiments, as we have just seen, regarding which international agencies ought to be taking the lead in filling the gaps that exist between emergency/refugee aid on one hand and longer term development aid on the other. In this regard, some marginal progress has been demonstrated in the cooperation between UNDP and UNHCR in Central America, while much less success and more problematic and complicated situations have prevailed in Africa. Arguments about handover from UNHCR to UNDP in cases of repatriation aid, in turn, betray & false assumption about development, i.e. that these agencies are the primary agents of such development. Our conceptual scheme emphasizes that handover from one international agency to another-is largely irrelevant. If the energies and aspirations of the local population are sufficiently engaged in the process of their own development, then "phase out" rather than "hand-over" 'is the appropriate mode in which international agencies should be operating.

The system of refugee aid and development that we propose in countries of asylum incorporates self-consciously many of the widely acknowledged principles mentioned above, while calling for the International Supervisory Agency (ISA) to take institutional control at the international level for allocation of resources, and it, the same time enlivening and promoting a system of development planning at the local level. We simply must get away from the notion that, development is done by international agencies. It is something that local people must do for themselves, and the international community's role is to provide judicious (not lavish) applications of resources to reward and catalyze local effort. The system of temporary protection described here embraces the principle that countries hosting large numbers of refugees should be provided assistance to compensate for both the humanitarian and developmental costs of asylum.

This is, we believe, important to preserving protection. Indeed, much of the compassion fatigue felt in recent years, both in countries of resettlement as well as in countries of first asylum, has to do with the sense that refugees may become a permanent drain on local resources. A system of temporary protection is one ameliorative to the restrictive tendencies inherent in this growing phenomenon of compassion fatigue. But an effective system of temporary protection must incorporate assistance components for host and stayee populations, as well as for refugees and returnees. Protection is linked with assistance.

But what are the appropriate modalities of assistance? The bulk of emergency and care and maintenance assistance should continue to be provided by the international community. Additionally, where refugee populations place burdens on local infrastructures (education, health, water supply, security systems, food storage, roads, environment, social services, range and land management, wood and energy supply, etc.), the host government and population should be provided assistance to compensate for these burdens and to strengthen the infrastructural capacity of refugee receiving areas. The effects of large refugee populations on local agriculture and employment should also be taken into account. But this compensation should be based on documented needs and it should be adequate to meeting just those tasks found most wanting. Money alone is not the key to development. The key is in stimulating, rewarding, and supporting initiative.

Several kinds of compensation to the host country should be taken into account to upgrade or initiate necessary infrastructures, This requires recognizing the needs of administration at the various levels of government:

(i) The central government should be compensated for strain placed on its transportation network and ports, for the additional costs of security and for other overhead costs;

(ii) The provincial governments should be compensated for strain placed on its transportation network, security costs, and for upgrading water supply and health facilities;

(iii) The district governments should be compensate for strain placed or, its transportation network, security costs, local health system, water supply, sanitation, food storage, environment, and extension services. In addition, special attention should be given to strengthening the district level managerial capacity.

Three kinds of international assistance are conceived as applying at these different levels. Humanitarian assistance for refugees is to be provided, initially, by the ISA through appropriate government ministries and local or expatriate NGOs. Most of this assistance should focus on meeting the emergency needs of refugees and, where appropriate, the local population, As a refugee situation moves beyond the emergency phase, it is assumed that humanitarian assistance will be gradually phased out and that ongoing assistance will be channelled through local institutions (see discussion infra regarding local and refugee development councils). A second form of assistance concerns infrastructure. Refugee flows have implications for infrastructure at the national, provincial, and district levels. We recommend that the ISA allocate in any given refugee situation fifty percent of these resources to the district level. Finally, an often forgotten cost concerns administration of refugee programmes. Where refugee flows raise administrative costs, these should be included in assistance, and special attention should be attached to the question of improving the management capacity and administrative absorptive capacity of national, provincial, and especially district level government.

The model we propose below attempts to address this problem of managerial capacity. In return for the assistance it will receive as a state of temporary asylum, the host country government agrees to a series of policies and procedures in terms of coping with the refugee population and preparing it for eventual return to the country of origin. The ISA *must be* prepared to work with each level of the host country government's administrative system in order to identify special infrastructural and development needs. Our assumption is that the greatest burdens on infrastructure will occur in those regions most directly impacted by the refugee presence.

Thus, the majority of infrastructural assistance should be allocated for strengthening of the district government level. To make this local application of resources and assistance work, it is essential not only that the line ministry representatives at the district level are involved in the planning and implementation of programmes, but also that the local population and the refugees are actively engaged. Indeed, the district government level of administration should be conceived as serving a coordinating function of planning and implementation undertaken by both local development councils and refugee development councils. One may conceive of these latter two bodies as being the fulcrum of effective development policy and eventual repatriation.

Large refugee flows are often conceptualized as development-depressing events, insofar as they impose development burdens. Often the refugee population is viewed as a supine recipient of charity, even as local populations, who may indeed suffer from so large a presence of refugees among them, are ignored. Refugee flows are conceived of as international events, in which the chief actors are the international agencies and foreign non-governmental agencies (NGOs) that work with the host government. This conception of refugee events ignores the fact that refugee and local populations, though often facing great exigency and stress, are quite resourceful. We believe that any new regime for temporary protection and facilitation of repatriation must take this fact into account.

Thus, from the very outset of a refugee event, we recommend that the international community shift the emphasis away from the international to the local. We propose that, prior to any funds being allocated for local infrastructural assistance, two local bodies be created: a Refugee Development Council (RDC) and a Local Development Council (LDC). The RDC should be composed of representatives of the newly arrived refugee population, including, where acceptable, community elders. Where appropriate, the RDC should be elected. Similarly, the LDCs should represent the economic, tribal, and geographical interests of the host country population. Though stressing traditional elder roles, RDCs and LDCs should be viewed as a means of identifying and unleashing skills that exist among the local and refugee populations, including the work of doctors and traditional healers, engineers and teachers, economists, and entrepreneurs. They should also be so composed as to reflect the special needs and interests of women. We recognize, in this connection, that some of the traditional leadership structures are undoubtedly unrepresentative and oppressive, but change, including gender-related change, ultimately must come from within. Outside intervention can only be facilitative. New organizations will often arise amid ongoing, if sometimes emaciated, traditional structures. Women are afforded new and sometimes liberating opportunities. These should be cultivated where possible by special ISA trust funds to encourage the productive participation of women, even as traditional authority structures are engaged in repatriation planning and development during the asylum phase. In short, the key in our view is to maximize local institutions and initiative, whether they be traditional or newly formed ones.

The formation of these councils assumes that the international community has already undertaken an initial survey of the refugee population to determine such things as the provinces of origin, reasons for flight, and the distribution of skills and vulnerabilities among the refugee population. However, one of the main functions of the RDC should be to refine this profile of the refugee population in preparation for eventual repatriation. We conceive of the LDC as having a similar responsibility in terms of identifying skills and vulnerabilities among the host population. The RDCs and LDCs, working singly and in cooperation with one another, will become the principal mechanisms through which humanitarian and development-related assistance will be channelled at the district level. Hence, such bodies are viewed as working directly with the district line ministries in terms of planning and implementing assistance activities.

As much as fifty percent of all infrastructural assistance should be funnelled through these councils, which in turn will select indigenous and expatriate NGO cooperative partners to assist in planning and implementation. The ISA should monitor and supervise these local planning and implementation efforts in conjunction with the host country government, but the principal thrust of planning and implementation is to remain at the local/district level. To ensure that monies are properly accounted for, the LDCs and RDCs would have staff accountants and be audited by an ISA accountant. Outside evaluations ought to be conducted and reports submitted to the ISA and the host country national government.

The model here by we proposed addresses a number of problems. First, while existing practice reflects the principle of organizing refugee camp populations into local governing bodies, these bodies equally often in practice deal only with routine matters of camp administration, and they answer to a UNHCR or government representative in the camp. Camps are usually treated as the unit of administration, and the refugee bodies therein have little or no responsibility for the planning and allocation of budgetary resources.

We conceive of the RDCs as providing not only an internal camp mechanism, but regional mechanisms for enhancing the repatriation of an entire refugee population to a particular country of origin. Moreover, the RDCs would be responsible for the planning of projects, the allocation of resources, and be held accountable for these activities. Similarly the LDCs would be expected to work with the RDCs in a joint LDC/RDC Committee to rationalize a regional development strategy that takes into account both refugee and host population interests and needs. Working together, under ISA supervision and with host government oversight, these bodies would be responsible for identifying skills among their respective populations and mobilizing these in cooperation with the government's district administration. Among the supervisory functions of the ISA country representative would be the resolution of disputes between the LDCs and RDCs. The result should be a blossoming of local planning capabilities and a reduction of the administrative absorptive capacity problem. Local and foreign NGOs engaged in the initial humanitarian response would join in the longer term rationalization of local development strategies, and be hired by the LDC/RDC coordinative body to bolster the local planning efforts and fill in where gaps in expertise are identified. Just as NGOs are required to have governmental approval to work in a country, so they would be required under this model to have permission from the LDC/RDC coordinative body to work in refugee-affected areas. This should ensure proper coordination of NGO activities, and further foster the development or local managerial capacity, LDC/RDC cooperation and coordination would be especially critical in resolving employment, fuel supply, health, water and sanitation issues, and in designing strategies to bolster such infrastructure.

RDCs and Preparation for Repatriation

The role of the RDCs is especially critical in readying the refugee population for successful repatriation. From the outset of a refugee flow, the ISA, NGOs and the host government should mobilize refugee populations into local and regional RDCs. The chief purpose of the RDCs is to work with the host LDCs to rationalize and implement humanitarian and development-related assistance at the local level, and with similar agencies and organizations in the country of origin. We conceive of the RDCs - under ISA supervision - playing an active role in pursuing confidence-building measures for repatriation. Activities in the country of origin are described in greater detail in the next section.

But it is important to emphasize here that successful preparation for eventual repatriation begins, in principle, the moment refugees enter a country of asylum, and that among the contacts that must be established and strengthened are ties with stayee organizations and local governments in the areas of eventual return.

Other functions of the RDC, apart from maintaining and deepening ties with local political structures in the home country, should include conducting surveys of the refugee population, reconstructing the community life of the refugees, engagement in local development planning, promoting development education, skills development, local repatriation investment activities, and repatriation education. Each of these activities is described in greater detail below. In the country of temporary protection, more particularly, the RDC would perform a number of important functions. The first priority for the RDC should be to complete and refine a survey of the refugee population to determine provinces of origin and the reasons for flight, to develop an V inventory or profile of refugee skills, and occupations, and to identify vulnerable groups in need of special assistance.

The international community routinely does this kind of work already. The data generated from such surveys is the baseline information that can be used to identify where assistance needs lie. It is essential in justifying and rationalizing assistance and in identifying a strategy and plan for eventual repatriation aid and development assistance. Documentation of need must proceed in tandem with reconstruction of the refugee community in temporary exile. A principal goal of the RDC is quickly to encourage the refugee population to reorganize itself in exile so as to address its immediate needs through self-reliant activity, and to begin the process of planning for repatriation. Foremost among the latter activities is the establishment of communication links with stayee organizations, so that information about conditions in the country of origin flows continually to refugees in exile. Once conditions of greater safety are realized, the RDC should, with ISA support, explore the fielding of repatriation planning teams to the country of origin for planning meetings with stayee organizations.

Equally important for the successful repatriation of the refugees is that they be engaged in learning new skills or upgrading old ones that will be usefully employed not only during the period of exile, but during the period of return. Such skills might include brick-making and laying, road building and repair work, forestation techniques, soil conservation, poultry raising and small animal husbandry, carpentry, water and well building technology, sanitation techniques, and health education. The promotion and upgrading of these kinds of vocational skills during a period of exile encourages a refugee population to contribute to the development of the host country, reduces reliance on external assistance, and paves the way for a more highly trained and skilled refugee population to return home where their energies and abilities can be turned to the reconstruction, rehabilitation, and development of their homelands.

Generally speaking, education in these skill areas should be provided in the refugee's home language, although an opportunity to learn a new language should not be looked upon as a burden by the refugee community. The attainment of new skills and upgrading of old ones can be achieved through a variety of means. The international community currently emphasizes vocational training, income generation, and food-for-work programmes funded by the UNHCR, the International Labour Organization (ILO), and WFP, often in conjunction with international NGOs. Many of these have desirable effects and they should be continued, although we suggest that the primary locus for planning and implementation of such programmes should be shifted to the RDCs in cooperation with the LDCs and the host country's local or district government officials. To the extent that refugee populations working in tandem with host country nationals identify, plan, and implement road-building projects, hospital or school construction projects, reforestation and soil conservation programmes, they will be using and learning new skills while helping to upgrade the local development situation in the region of asylum.

Such programmes enhance a sense of goodwill between the refugee and host population, provide income to refugees which reduces reliance on direct charity, promote the strengthening of host country infrastructure, and build a reservoir of trained workers among refugees that can be tapped to facilitate successful reconstruction and rehabilitation efforts upon return to the country of origin. Thus, one may we recommend that infrastructure programmes supported by external funds rely wherever possible on refugee and host country labour, use local building materials, rely on local building techniques, and that these programmes should be managed by local organizations rather than expatriate ones. Of necessity, most such projects should be of a smaller and more manageable scale relying on technologies and techniques that are not overly capital intensive or heavily dependent on the importation of non-indigenous materials or of non-indigenous expertise.

In this connection, the idea of Quick Impact Projects (QIPs), first devised for returnee areas in Central America, and conceived as a useful tool in bridging from short-term aid to a longer-term development orientation in countries of origin, could also be usefully employed in the first of asylum.

QIPs that are imposed phases of refugee flows into countries from above stand little chance of achieving sustainability.

Therefore, RDCs and LDCs should take the -lead in designing and implementing such programmes, relying on local or expatriate NGOs where they see a need for complementary support from such sources. Better yet, we propose that the RDCs and LDCs focus on developing (SLIPs), rather than QIPs as such. Most contemporary assistance promoting income generation, food-for-work, and vocational training pays lip service to the notion of refugee or host country population participation in management of programmes. Our view is that ultimate authority and real responsibility for design, implementation, and management of these programmes should lie with the affected populations. They should not be seen as merely participating in such activities, but should actually have the authority to devise them and make them work. International involvement, should be strictly facilitative, both in terms work. International involvement should be strictly facilitative, both in terms of providing seed money and in terms of advising and complementing local efforts. The RDCs and LDCs should take the lead in planning, and be held accountable through audits and reports, as would any public body entrusted with fiduciary responsibilities.

Another form of education that often will be central to the security of a refugee population upon its return to the country of origin is mine detection and mine awareness education. Where this is a relevant concern, RDCs should be tasked with the creation of mine detection teams among the refugee population even during the period of temporary asylum. Here the international community can usefully provide experts to train the refugee population in simple techniques and provide the necessary equipment for mine detection. Once a body of mine detectors is trained, it should also be tasked with promotion mine awareness and be actively engaged through the tasked with promotion mine awareness and be actively engaged through the RDC in developing ties with the local bodies in the country of origin to identify mine-littered zones, and to make sure that they are marked and mapped for eventual attention.

An effective system for returnee aid and development must be linked with ongoing strategies for repatriation in the country of temporary protection. It must take into account the fast-changing reality of global politics, the indivisibility of the processes of repatriation, reconstruction, development and peacemaking, the capability of displaced people to reconstruct their own communities, and the right of people to return to their country or place of origin in conditions of safety and dignity. Since the early 1990s, the UNHCR has been experimenting with innovative and creative reintegration projects in countries of return, such as Nicaragua, Cambodia, Afghanistan, Ethiopia, and Mozambique.

These experiments represent a major shift in the right direction, but they are far from addressing the central questions of reconstruction and recovery. Hurdles include the organization's limited mandate, funding arrangements, and problems in enforcing the so-called inter-agency cooperative solutions. Although it is rarely admitted, the so-called inter-agency (UNHCR/UNDP) cooperative solutions are seldom considered by the two parties equally worthwhile. This is exacerbated by their inability to develop effective and low cost enforcement of agreements. In view of this institutional impasse, an attempt at reconceptualization of the existing international refugee regime is in order. The aim should not be, however, to tear down what has been built during the last four decades, but to build on past achievements and move forward to face the challenge ushered in by the end of the Cold War.

Two key elements constitute the central plank of this reformed regime. First, we must seek to fill the gap in the existing organizational framework caused by an unhelpful division in the conceptualization of relief and development. The organization that is designed, among other things, to fill this lacuna should be able to work with refugee, returnees, internally displaced and poor residents throughout the whole, process of emergency, reconstruction, peacemaking and development, without being fettered by any constitutional (mandate) constraints. Second, the fundamental principle underlying the new regime should be the right of people to return in conditions of honour and safety to their countries, or to areas to which they are culturally attached. In this framework, refugeehood is perceived as a transient phenomenon for which voluntary repatriation is the ultimate solution. This presupposes that new aid strategies which emphasize human rights, peace settlement and reconciliation conditionalities are developed to address the root and proximate causes of displacement, and to allow those in exile to return home. Unlike the present system which is reactive, the new regime should be proactive.

This may involve using economic sanctions and other forms of constraints to bring pressure to bear on regimes which lack respect for human rights. In exceptional cases, it may even involve a certain degree of encroachment on state sovereignty, inasmuch as the state impinges upon the right of people to remain or to return in safety. The concepts of temporary protection and early repatriation do not make sense without this link. In most cases, addressing root causes and refractory regimes in countries of return can be undertaken through a combination of diplomatic pressure, economic sanctions, and material incentives, without resorting to more coercive military measures.

Voluntary Repatriation as the Optimal Solution

Voluntary repatriation takes place under a variety of different conditions. Refugees may return to (i) an on-going armed conflict (Cuny, et al, 1992), (ii) countries where there has been no change of government, but where there have been declarations of general amnesty; (iii) situations where there has been a change of government; (iv) newly-born states where the states in question may have no responsibility for causing the displacement of the returning refugees; or (vi) defunct states. Each case scenario requires different modalities of intervention. Assuming the conditions in the country of asylum are not unbearable, there are two elements which fundamentally influence the decision of refugees to repatriate, namely security and the prospects of economic survival. However, not only is the concept of safety elusive, but absolute safety is seldom attainable.

Even though most safe conditions can be gauged or are amenable to objective measurement, sometimes countries that appear to be unsafe to outsiders may have enclaves which are safe enough to allow return. If this Were not the case, very few people would return to conditions of pervasive conflict, and yet we know that many do. Refugees' are rational decision-makers. Thus, unless the conditions in the countries of asylum are impossible, even small numbers of returnees are an indication of either the existence of safe areas within the troubled country, or of refugee agreements with feuding parties for safe passage and abode.

Generally, refugees are in the best position to know when to return. The function of outsiders should be to facilitate their decision. This; however, is an elusive role.

Refugees in camps or reception centres are often, unfortunately, dependent on hand-outs donated by outsiders. A reduction of such assistance, lack of opportunities outside these sites, or legal restrictions on freedom of movement and residence have often left refugees with no choice but to return to unfavourable conditions. This can be illustrated partially by the example of Afghan refugees in Pakistan who relinquished their passbooks in return for a repatriation grant (encashment). Between May and October of 1992. nearly 900,000 refugees were observed crossing the border into Afghanistan.

Even though there is no clear evidence to show that deregistration was the only factor that triggered return to unfavourable conditions characterized by an ongoing civil war, the fact that UNHCR and the host government initiated the encashment (deregistration) programme to facilitate return is problematical, especially since a large number of the returnees have for the second time fled their country to seek asylum in Pakistan, and have been refused entry because the Pakistani border is closed to new arrivals. As practice currently stands, the question is whether return to unfavourable political conditions should be facilitated, discouraged, or opposed. This depends on whether there is a clear and imminent danger to the safety of returnees. The UNHCR, for example, after initially supporting repatriation efforts, withdrew its support for the repatriation of Rwandese refugees from Zaire after it became clear that returnees were subjected to arbitrary killing. Where, however, there are safe enclaves within the country concerned and refugees are given an assurance that they will be able to reenter the country of asylum should conditions in the country of origin deteriorate, the decision of refugees to return should be respected and assistance provided to facilitate their return and reintegration into their former communities.

The major assumption underlying the new regime is that refugees will eventually return to their country of origin. Consequently, the groundwork for return must begin in the country of asylum from the beginning of an emergency programme even when there is an on-going pervasive war. Under conditions of careful preparation for voluntary repatriation, in which the refugees are involved from the very start, there should be fewer cases where refugees are subjected to coercive repatriation. They will not be surviving on hand-cuts in the country of temporary asylum, but rather developing resourceful communities in anticipation of return. Thus, assistance to any refugee programme should be oriented towards solutions, and every available opportunity should be seized to facilitate spontaneous returns with the aim of reducing the size of the refugee population without compromising the safety of returnees.

One of the major weaknesses of the present international regime is that refugees are seldom offered an alternative to bleak existence in camps. This can be illustrated by the example of the Cambodian refugees who resided along the Thai border. A recent UNHCR evaluation report concluded that the repatriation operation of the border population might have been less intensive, less complex, and less costly, if the assistance programme in Thailand had been solution-oriented from an earlier date. This stud further pointed out that:

> "a significant potential for spontaneous returns existed prior to the signing of the Paris accords, but no efforts were made to facilitate such movement. Instead of seeking a steady reduction in the size of the border population, the international community preferred to sustain a situation in which the refugees were effectively deprived of viable alternatives to life in the camps."

Under the principles inhering in the regime we propose here, condition in the country of temporary protection will focus on the development needs of the host country, and the ultimate reintegration of the refugee population into an improved development context in the country of origin. Far from increasing the arbitrary nature of voluntary repatriation as it has often been experienced in the past decade, such a system should at once reduce pressures for repatriation from the government of temporary protection and increase incentives for return.

But all this hinges on the willingness of governments to accept a new system of principles and procedures that are solution-oriented that aggressively promote peaceful resolution of disputes in countries, of -origin, that promote the expansion of local development capacity, and that are backed by adequate financial support. Development is defined as "the unfolding of "what is there," a realization of human potential and expansion of capabilities. Any meaningful developmental intervention should therefore begin with a correct assessment of existing vulnerabilities, potentialities, and capabilities. Present programmes are often formulated in the dark because they take little cognizance of these elements.

Refugees, especially at the initial stage, are said to be traumatized and are assumed to lack the motivation and energy to take initiative based on a correct understanding of their situation (for a critique of this approach, see Kibreab, 1994). There is a tendency among all concerned, including academics, to extrapolate from other experiences, rather than treat every situation as different and as having its own dynamics. This does not deny the fact that there are certain predictable aspects in refugee situations, but rather recognizes that the success of outside intervention is not determined by the ability to understand generalities, but by the ability to grasp particulars. To overcome this weakness, whenever a refugee crisis arises a solution oriented survey should be undertaken to identify the refugees' areas of origin (provinces, districts and villages, including homesteads), reasons for flight, property left behind (land, house, livestock, money, other types of property), skills profile, social networks, leadership structure, vulnerable population groups, and the like. Such surveys could be undertaken, with ISA supervision, by academics at local universities in the countries of origin or return. It is necessary to replicate the survey in villages of origin so that some of the factors that caused displacement can be systematically addressed, and the property refugees left behind could be protected, not by using the coercive forces of the state, but by providing incentive structure that, sustain and strengthen existing institutions - customs and normative rules - regulating property rights and other forms of social interactions at district and/or village levels.

These institutions are the major sources of social harmony, and their collapse is the most important source of conflict that prompts people to flee, prevents those in exile from returning, or those who have returned from being anchored into their previous socio-cultural setting in conditions of safety and dignity. To a large extent, in countries such as Somalia, Sierra Leone, Liberia, Sudan, Cambodia, and Afghanistan, it is the collapse of the moral authority of elders, resource-regulating institutions (traditional values, norms, customs, and normative rules) and enforcement mechanisms that forced people to flee, and prevented those in exile from returning.

These institutional constraints are socially transmitted, and are an essential part of the cultural heritage of rural societies. Community reconstruction in wartorn societies should begin with reconstructing traditional institutions and enforcement mechanisms which are the sine qua non of social harmony. Unfortunately, however, this critical aspect is often overlooked.

Identification of vulnerabilities and capabilities of returnees, stayees and internally displaced persons is also critical for planning, designing, and implementing programmer that build on and expand existing capacities. This is essential for sustainable self sufficiency and reintegration. programmes in countries of asylum and return. Since the ultimate solution to the refugee problem is voluntary repatriation, the objective of the developmental activities both in countries of temporary protection return should be to strengthen and reinforce the institutional, organizational, technical, and management capabilities of refugees, returnees, and residents.

Country of Origin

Planning for repatriation should begin at the very outset of a refugee situation. Indeed, much of what has been discussed above can be initiated early on. However, when there is a sign of improvement in the security situation in the country of origin, even more aggressive efforts to prepare and initiate repatriation movements should be undertaken. In most Third World countries, improvement or deterioration in security is inextricably linked with development or lack of it. In these countries, where displacement is a result of an interplay between political, economic, social, cultural, and environmental factors as well as ethnic disharmony, a well thought-out developmental intervention at the national, provincial, district, and village levels could gradually create the necessary conditions for voluntary repatriation. In most of the refugee-producing countries, especially in Africa, it is the inability of the state to fulfil its most rudimentary functions that is the cause of breakdown in social order. This is reflected in the collapse of the infrastructure, breakdown in law and order, and lack of control over territories and resources.

The first step in any country repatriation planning should be a meeting between representatives of refugee communities, stayees, and internally displaced persons to start the process of reconciliation, healing, confidence building, and settlement of property rights. If possible, residents' representatives should also reciprocate by visiting the refugees in their country of asylum. If refugees have been away for many years, it is likely that most of their property will have been taken by those, who stayed behind. If the latter are required to relinquish these interests, they may resent the idea of receiving returnees. Development assistance as identified by both the stayees and returnees should therefore be provided by the International Supervisory Agency (ISA) to accommodate the new demands, and to offset the loss of assets that may be suffered by the resident population. If this happens, returnees may be considered an asset rather than a burden. Ideally, such contact will have the approval of the government and/or rebel groups in the country of origin. Even where this is not so, opposing parties should, under the new refugee regime, understand that communication between refugee and stayee groups at the local level will take place under.

Once the security situation has improved, more aggressive pursuit of development of joint refugee/stayee contacts should be undertaken. At this stage, identification of SLIP projects that address security concerns, transportation, food storage capacity, and land and property dispute resolution should also be initiated. Upon restoration of peace, full-fledged implementation of repatriation should begin along with specific steps to encourage full reintegration of returnees. The emphasis at this point should be on Identifying food surpluses from among the stayee population that could be purchased by the ISA and/or by returning refugees. In addition, integration of the RDCs with the LDCs in the country of origin should be effected, and steps taken to promote security at the local level through village watch programmes. It is to a discussion of the integration aid strategy at this last stage of the restoration of peace that we now turn.

At a national level, the main focus of reconstruction aid should be on democratization, economic growth, institution-building, training programmes, and job creation. Key to all these is an institutional framework which provides a favourable incentive structure to economic and political actors, which should include foreign investors. Since these efforts would be futile in the absence of peace, it is essential for the ISA to tie its' financial and technical assistance to compliance with peace agreements, strict observance of minimum standards of human rights, and willingness to undertake policy and institutional reforms. In some countries - Guatemala, for example - the success of voluntary repatriation is inextricably linked to issues relating to land tenure systems. Thus, another prerequisite of ISA support should be the reform of land policies.

The effectiveness of development assistance is to a large extent a function of efficient, incorruptible, and adequate administrative capacity. Most countries of return lack the necessary administrative capacity to absorb a substantial amount of assistance. Generous assistance to countries without adequate administrative capacity may further aggravate the level of inefficiency and corruption. It is therefore necessary to build administrative capacities at the national, provincial, and district levels. This should be accomplished through providing relevant training schemes, preferably using locally available skills. Outside technical assistance should be kept to a minimum. Only when there are no qualified nationals available should the services of outside experts be tapped, and their involvement should be phased out after national counterparts are trained.

It is important to point out, however, that capacity-building is neither a panacea, nor can it be achieved in a vacuum. Lack of institutional capacity and the existence of corruption and inefficiency, are indicative of wider social and economic problems, and cannot be eliminated overnight through outside intervention. That is why the aim of ISA intervention should be partly to enhance the ability of refugee populations to demand change in their governance, and partly to soften the grip of the state by subjecting it to different kinds of pressures, so that it becomes responsive to its citizens demands. On top of investment in human, policy, and institutional development, it is important to invest in development of the physical and social infrastructures in order to accommodate increased demands and to improve available services. For example, delivery of aid to a large number of returnees and internally displaced persons may strain available physical facilities such as roads, and port and transport facilities.

Central governments in countries of return should be compensated for the wear and tear on roads and of port facilities. It is also important to invest in strengthening the judiciary, police force, and organs of civil society, such as indigenous nongovernmental organizations (for example, associations of farmers, nomads, youths women, workers, and students). Provided the state in question is democratic, and there are safeguards against the possibility of using the coercive forces of the state for suppression of its citizens' rights, it may be useful to strengthen the capacity of the state to protect lives and property. In many countries of return, the inability of the state to maintain law and order is one of the important factors which leads to new outflows. The presence of an accountable state which is able to fulfil rudimentary functions such as control over territory, maintenance of law and order, and supply of basic services is a prerequisite to successful and permanent repatriation.

Remarkably, Similar assistance programmes should also be implemented in the provinces to which refugees return. Even though the kind of assistance needed by different provinces in different countries is likely to vary depending on the level of available infrastructure and extent of damage experienced, it will often be necessary to build or upgrade schools, hospitals, roads, water supply systems, bridges, sanitation facilities, etc. In order to improve the food security situation, storage facilities should also be constructed using locally available skills and materials.

Now we will look at contemporary status of international efforts for refrugee/returnee aid and development.

12

International Efforts for Refugee/ Returnee Aid and Development

It is pertinent to note that There is a built-in "exilic" bias in the way solutions to the refugee problem are conceptualized in the international instruments relating to refugee status (with the exception of the 1969 OAU Convention). Solutions are conceived within the context of exile, i.e. short of changes that may occur in countries of origin. There is an historical explanation for this. The international refugee regime was developed in the heyday of the Cold War as an instrument of Western countries' foreign policies.

Infact, the overwhelming proportion of those persons who sought international protection originated from the then-Communist countries or their satellite states, where political change in the refugees' lifetime was considered improbable. Two of the three standard solutions to the refugee problem, namely settlement in countries of first asylum and resettlement in third countries were, therefore, initially designed and implemented to address the needs of post-World War II Europe where voluntary repatriation remained only a most distant hope, if a hope at all. At the end of World War II, Europe's loss of productive assets, namely labour and capital, was huge.

About forty million civilians and military personnel had been killed, and another thirty-five million were believed to have been wounded during the war. The situation was also exacerbated by demographic distortions owing to gender imbalances and by a shortage of the productive age groups. Although the European economies were in a state of chaos at the end of the war, the economic reconstruction and recovery experienced by all the affected countries was dramatic. By 1950, Western Europe had regained or surpassed the pre-war output levels. Between 1950 and 1970, GDP grew at an average of about 53 percent per annum, and the rate of growth of industrial production was over seven percent for the same period.

This growth continued uninterrupted until 1974 when recession set in following the 1972-73 economic boom. The standard solutions to refugee situations were developed during this period when the economies of the receiving countries experienced unprecedented economic expansion in the context of depleted populations. Two key elements facilitated this rapid economic recovery and reconstruction: the technical and financial assistance provided by the United States under the Marshall Plan, and the heavy influx of refugees and expellees which offset the losses of manpower. Between 1947 and 1952, Europe received $US 22.5 billion under the Marshall Plan alone, of which $US 19.7 billion was donated in the form of gifts.

The process of post-war recovery was further facilitated by the creation of three important organizations, namely the International Monetary Fund (IMF), the International Bank for Reconstruction and Development (IBRD) following the Bretton Woods negotiations in 1944, and the General Agreement on Tariffs and Trade (GATT) in 1947. These organizations were established to promote international economic cooperation in the areas of credit, monetary and trade policy. The aid provided by the United States under the Marshall Plan and other similar schemes, combined with the need for reconstruction of the economic and social infrastructure, created a demand for labour.

Thus, refugees and expellees were either readily absorbed into countries of first arrival or were accepted for resettlement in the United States, Canada, Australia and New Zealand where there was an abundant demand for labour. The important role played by the refugees and expellees in the economic recovery of several of the European countries is emphasized by several researchers. The social, economic, and political realities accompanying the refugee situation in Africa, Asia, and Central America today are considerably different-from the economic and Political reality, as well as the humanitarian solidarity, that existed in post-World War II Europe. Unlike the latter, today's refugee problem in the Third World is taking place in the context of serious structural problems, unresolved political and military conflicts indebtedness, lower primary commodity prices and declining export earnings, reduced net capital flows and high population growth. The situation is further complicated by the demise of the Cold War, which eliminated the strategic significance of refugees and exacerbated donor compassion fatigue.

This reality notwithstanding, solutions to the Third World refugee problem continue to be conceptualized within the context of exile. The central question which one should ask, then, is whether the so-called durable solutions established in the immediate post-World War period are still viable. Can the refugee problem today be solved within the context of exile when the economies of the countries of first asylum are plunged into deep crises, and when the countries in the West seem, in effect, to be closing their doors to asylum-seekers? There is little doubt that the problems prompting displacement are many and varied, and thus, that there cannot be a universally valid solution applicable to all refugee situations.

Infact, the old tripartite set of solutions may still be serviceable but reliance on local settlement, and third country resettlement, with minimal emphasis, politically or financially, on voluntary repatriation, no longer accords with changing political, economic, and attitudinal conditions at both the regional and global levels. Strategies and policies that do not change in response to changing circumstances are likely to wither and die, and we may have reached such a pass in contemporary international relations concerning refugees. Thus, some rethinking of the traditional solutions, and of the exilic bias inherent in them, is in order if the institution of asylum one of the twentieth century's finest achievements is to be salvaged.

One of the first steps that needs to be undertaken is to rid the international refugee regime of its "exilic" bias. Apart from exceptional cases, solutions to the refugee problem should be conceptualized along an exile-repatriation continuum. The advantage of this dynamic approach is that exile is conceptualized as a transient phenomenon or as a springboard to a permanent solution. If exile is considered a temporary solution, it will be imperative to design and implement assistance programmes that are solution-oriented from the outset. Assistance programmes in the country of asylum should be designed to fulfil a dual function: on the one hand, to enable refugees to become self-supporting (in exile) and, on the other, to create technical, management and social skills by building on existing indigenous knowledge and social organizations that will contribute to their reintegration upon return.

Unlike the immediate post-World War II period, at present the conditions that allow voluntary repatriation are not a sole function of cessation of persecution or conflict. Economic deprivation and destruction of the social and economic infrastructure by war can discourage refugees from returning in spite of changed political circumstances. The Eritrean refugees in Sudan are a classic example of this phenomenon.

But, until recently, the bulk of UNHCR assistance programmes were almost exclusively channelled to countries of asylum, This was a continuation of the way in which solutions to the refugee problem the world over were perceived by those who drafted the international instruments relating to the status of refugees and by the states that subsequently ratified them. Whenever UNHCR was involved in voluntary repatriation, its programmes focused on individual returnees, rather than on the communities and the areas to which they returned.

Assistance consisted of a short-term grant of food, a cash travel allowance, roofing materials, basic farming tools, and household utensils. Reintegration was primarily considered the responsibility of the home country, and was expected to occur spontaneously. It was assumed that governments in the countries of origin, in collaboration with development agencies, would meet the needs of these communities in the context of national development programmes. However, since the demise of the Cold War, there has been a growing awareness within the international community of the need to shift emphasis from exile to voluntary repatriation. The UNHCR is playing a vanguard role in this. Not only has there been a shift of emphasis, but repatriation is no longer conceptualized in terms of physical transfer of refugees from the countries of asylum to the countries of origin. It is looked at as a process of reimplanting uprooted communities into their previous socio-cultural milieu in conditions of safety and dignity, where the root and proximate causes of poverty and displacement are addressed. This is a worthwhile shift because only now can repatriation be an empowering and irreversible process. This fresh approach was precipitated, on the one hand, by the sense of optimism ushered in by the decay of Communism, which unleashed un-precedented hopes for the potential resolution of many refugee situations the world over and, on the other, by the realization of the high degree of infrastructural destruction in the countries of return.

Apart from their destroyed social and economic infrastructure and limited -absorptive capacity, areas of likely repatriation are frequently littered with land mines which are a threat to physical and subsistence security of the returning populations. Moreover, in war-torn societies returnees are only a sub-set of larger disrupted societies "Whose communities cannot be rebuilt in isolation from other disadvantaged groups, such as the internally displaced, poor residents, demobilized combatants and their families.

It is pertinent to note that the UNHCR is openly questioning the assumptions which underlay its past approaches to returnee assistance and reintegration. For example, the Executive Committee of the High Commissioner's Programme stated that the assumptions which underpinned the organization's past returnee assistance strategy have largely proved ill-founded, and it has become clear that there exists a serious gap between relief assistance and development programmes. This gap not only threatens the successful reintegration of returnees in terms of their ability to remain home and to rebuild their lives, it also threatens the viability of the communities.

This suggests that unless the "gap" is bridged, firstly,

returnees will be unable to anchor themselves in their areas of origin without having to flee once more to urban centres or to a neighbouring country in search of livelihood; secondly, the returning populations will be unable to reconstruct their communities in a sustainable manner; and thirdly, reconciliation between returnees, stayees, internally displaced and demobilized former combatants or soldiers will be impossible if they have to compete for scarce resources in the context of rising numbers of newly transplanted people. Competition for extremely scarce resources between groups that played different roles during the conflict that prompted displacement could lead to renewed recrimination and civil strife.

In extreme situations, this could lead to open conflict undermining the dividends of a fragile peace in the making. The Executive Committee identifies three critical elements that should be addressed to bridge the "gap" between emergency relief and development, These are increased and sustained inter-agency cooperation, innovative models of assistance that enhance reintegration, and inclusion of areas of return in national plans of development.

Inter-Agency Cooperation

Remarkably, the call for increased inter-agency cooperation in the area of development oriented refugee aid is as old as the latter concept itself and, unfortunately, both the approach and the call have failed abysmally to achieve many tangible results. Moreover, there is little hope that the call will yield better results in the foreseeable future because the institutional dichotomy between those who are concerned with humanitarian assistance, e.g. UNHCR, and those concerned with development aid, e.g. UNDP, is, within the given constitutional divisions of responsibility, unbridgeable. The first call for increased inter-agency cooperation in the design and implementation of a development-oriented assistance strategy to refugees and refugee-affected areas was made during the Conference on the Assistance to African Refugees held in Addis Ababa (Ethiopia) in 1967. One of the recommendations concerning refugee aid adopted by the Conference was that it is desirable to ensure as early as possible ... the assistance of those members of the UN family which normally participate in the later development activities, including WFP, UNDP, ECA, UNICEF, FAO, ILO, WHO and UNESCO. This call was made twenty-seven years ago, and it has been repeated with varying emphasis in nearly every relevant international forum since.

Still, the gulf between the activities undertaken by humanitarian organizations and development organizations remains wide. The failure of inter-agency cooperation in development-oriented refugee-returnee assistance programmes relates at least in part to the nature of the division of tasks, working methods, priorities, operational structures and institutional cultures between and among the UN sister organizations.

Every agency in the UN system is designed to deal with specific tasks. It their tasks were easily interchangeable, there would have been no rationale for the creation of the different organizations. Recognizing this, we are also faced with the problem that many of the agencies have overlapping responsibilities, which only intensifies the turf sensibilities of each agency. Thus, while inter-agency coordination is desperately needed, many obstacles impede its realization.

Hitherto, the only tangible inter-agency cooperation in matters relating to refugees has been between UNHCR and WFP, and this is mainly attributable to the affinity of their constitutional responsibilities. The plea for UNHCR/ UNDP cooperation has produced only marginal progress. A recent

UNHCR evaluation report, for example, stated that UNHCR in its search for a partner that could complement its own mandate approached the UNDP and some other agencies. But even though some fruitful collaborative efforts were undertaken in the context of the International Conference on Central American Refugees (CIREFCA), "UNDP did not become a true complement to UNHCR in the refugee aid and development initiative". Although UNHCR and UNDP seemed to recognize that their activities could complement one another in addressing the inter-related issues of displacement, peace and development, as predicted earlier, "[differences in the two organizations' structure and style . . often hindered the implementation of the policy commitment. .." Another evaluation report also points out that when the quick impact projects (QIPs) were first initiated in Nicaragua within the framework of CIREFCA, it was hoped that a dose partnership would be established between UNHCR and the other UN agencies, especially UNDP, and that QIP-type projects could be "replicated in bilateral, multilateral or governmental programmes, at regional and national levels." In practice, however, the expectations regarding UNDP's role in the QIP programme have not been fulfilled. UNDP's role in the Joint Technical Team and in other aspects of the QIP initiative was "very marginal".

The report further points out that the advantages that can be gained from UNHCR' UNDP cooperation are so clear that the degree to which it actually takes place is often exaggerated in public statements and documents. This tendency is particularly evident in Central America, where the whole CIREFCA process is based on the notion that the two organization's can and do work closely. In practice, the different mandates, objectives, organizational cultures and working methods of UNHCR and UNDP have made it extremely difficult for the two organizations to collaborate.

This pattern is discernible everywhere. For example, although there were some improvements in UNHCR/UNDP collaborative efforts in the Cambodia repatriation operation, there were still problems emanating from the usual differences in outlook, mandate, and priorities. A recent evaluation report on the Cambodia repatriation operation states that the reintegration programme underlined the need for a more intensive dialogue between the two organizations (UNHCR and UNDP) in order to "address some philosophical differences which continue to impede effective collaboration". UNDP is a planning and technical assistance agency working with member governments in areas relating to national development, but it is not a development implementing agency, even though its Office of Special Projects (OSP) implements some projects.

UNHCR is a humanitarian organization which implements its programmes through government line ministries or nongovernmental organizations, and is sometimes at odds with governments when rights of refugees against government action or inaction. In Central America, these differences led to clashes between the two agencies. Their approaches are also different in the sense that UNHCR favours rapid implementation and achievement of concrete results, as opposed to UNDP's focus on longer-term planning and sustainability. This suggests that the call made by the UNHCR's Executive Committee for increased and sustained inter-agency cooperation in reintegration programmes is unlikely to yield tangible results. It is high time, therefore, that an alternative workable institutional arrangement be devised or some of the existing arrangements are expanded to fill the institutional gap. Organizations are developed in response to the need to overcome given constraints and there is no controversy as to the seriousness of the institutional constraints that exist in the area of refugee/returnee aid and development.

Now the question arise—Is there a "gap" between emergency relief and development? The answer is inextricably tied to the question about how we define development. Sen's (1989) and Ghai's (1989) definitions of development as capability expansion in which human "life is seen as a set of "doings and beings" called "functionings" which relate the "evaluation of the quality of life to the assessment of the capability to function" are quite helpful in this regard. Sen sees several "functionings" as constitutive of a person's being. These include "such elementary functionings as escaping morbidity and mortality, being adequately nourished, undertaking usual movements etc., to many complex functionings such as self-respect, taking part in the life of the community and appearing in public without shame".

Emergency relief is provided to restore depleted human energy and dignity which are sine qua non for the realization of human potential and expansion of human capabilities. Properly administered, emergency relief restores physical strength and human dignity and creates the necessary conditions for capability to function. This is not only an essential means to development', but also the ultimate goal of development. Much discussion of these' matters suffers from a lack of clarity and from an overemphasis on a false premise, namely that the gap exists between emergency relief and development, when in reality the gap is essentially organizational. Emergency relief interventions are intended to enable refugees to avoid hunger and escape death.

This indeed is a developmental intervention, but if it is provided in a context where there are no opportunities for engaging in productive activities, which are essential elements in the process of capability expansion (development), the effect of emergency relief can be counterproductive. However, because of the institutional gap in the existing international assistance regime, the developmental process set in motion by the provision of emergency relief is usually nipped in the bud. As a result, sustenance of lives, instead of enhancement of capabilities to function independently after initial enabling intervention, becomes the raison d'etre of emergency relief. In most emergency relief operations, the supply of goods and services is taken as an end in itself, and not as a means to set in motion the process of emancipation from the "enforced necessity to live less or be less," to borrow Sen's insightful language. If, in fact, the end of emergency relief becomes keeping refugees or other recipients alive without regard to the reconstruction and repair of their communities so that they can function fully after a disruptive experience in their lives, the supply of goods and services could, instead of catalyzing recovery, become the cause of disfranchisement, powerlessness and resignation. Whether refugees sink into the fantasy of idealizing the past by denying the present, or manage to take charge of the process of their recovery is, to a large extent, influenced by the nature of the outside intervention.

Innovative Models: Shortcomings

The innovative models devised by UNHCR to bridge the "gap" between relief and development are the Quick impact Projects (QIPs), in which humanitarian agencies are directed to work from the "relief end of the continuum while UNDP and other development agencies work from the development end". This approach, no matter how desirable, is fraught with the same difficulties discussed earlier, namely the two organizations' different operational structures and institutional cultures, which cannot be wished away even at the behest of mutual agreements.

The QIPs approach is innovative insofar as it is cost-effective, small-scale, uses local resources, and is gender-focused. There are, however, certain weaknesses associated with the approach. First, the major aim of QIP is to achieve quick results.

QIPs are even referred to as "emergency development." Development, especially a community-based development involving local participation, is a slow process to which haste in implementation is an anathema. QIPs are by definition, therefore, not usually the expression of community-based development, but are projects' largely imposed from outside and above, which seek community involvement in terms of needs identification and labour contribution. The outcome of consultations is invariably predictable because those local persons consulted by outsiders are usually the powerful and the articulate community members, and their needs are seldom identical to those of the silent, impoverished majority. The method of expression of the latter is whispering and not shouting, and those who are in a hurry, e.g. administrators of QIPs, have no time to listen for whispers.

It is only by adopting a learning process approach that one is able to understand what communities' needs are, and it is only by studying how communities interact with the natural environment and with each other that one can identify capacities and vulnerabilities. Any project imposed from above without having a clear understanding of how it will overcome vulnerabilities and expand capabilities is likely to be ineffective, if not counterproductive. Community-based development is initiated by the community concerned, and the aim of outside development assistance should be to enhance and consolidate community initiatives. This does not deny the existence of a situation in which potentially capable communities may, by force of circumstances, be incapacitated and prevented from resourcefully pursuing their own development. Clearly, refugees, returnees, internally displaced persons, and other marginalized groups cannot pursue development without some assistance. A worthwhile development assistance programme is one which enables people, even in these marginalized situations, to realize and expand their- potential. Development, as Chesterton once defined it, is the "unfolding of what is there" (quoted in German. 1993c). Most of the failures in development have been due to the failure to see "what is there," or to the false assumption that there is nothing there, and hence the ingredients should be brought from outside the communities concerned.

> ". . . people cannot be developed; they can only develop themselves. For while it is possible for an outsider to build a man's house, an outsider cannot give the man pride and self-confidence in himself as a human being, Those things a man has to create in himself by his own actions."

This task is a slow process and is far beyond UNHCR's mandate, because its involvement in reintegration activities should, according to its own understanding, not exceed two years. Two years, however, is too short a period for undertaking any meaningful development activity.

Second, the QIPs approach does not also address the thorny problems of recurrent costs and sustainability which have always been the Achilles' heel of UNHCR's assistance programmes, not only in relation to reintegration programmes in countries of return, but also in self-sufficiency projects in countries of first asylum. This weakness is by no means a result of lack of vision or direction on the part of UNHCR. On the contrary, within its limited institutional framework, UNHCR has been trying innovatively to adapt to new situations either by the flexible use of its limited mandate or by seeking authority from governments. Rather, it is a reflection, on the one hand, of the outer limit of the Office's mandate, and, on the other, of the institutional gap that characterizes the present international assistance regime. The key strategy suggested to overcome this is to link the emergency network represented by UNHCR to the development network represented by UNDP".

This is an unrealistic expectation because the available evidence suggests that when the time to phase out UNHCR's involvement comes, there is no one willing to carry on. Faced with financial and managerial problems, the self-sufficiency projects and QIPs often collapse. This may sound like a "prophecy of gloom," but the problem is already felt in Somalia. Ethiopia and in Cambodia and Nicaragua, where QIPs have been said to be most successful. In the Somali cross-border operation, lack of funds towards the end of 1993 brought the "activities [QIPs] to a standstill....

The persistent lack of funding has reduced cross-border activities to a minimum and with the still missing development agencies the future of activities is unpredictable." QIPs implemented within the Cross Mandate framework in Eastern Ethiopia are also faced with serious problems of sustainability (personal interview, 1994). According to people from the field, UNHCR is forced to keep QIPs going because the structure is unsustainable. In Nicaragua, according to UNHCR's plan, the regional Programmes of Assistance to Returnees (PARs) were expected to become the "field extension of PRN [the government's Programme for National Reconstruction], not only for the QIPs in 1992, but for the PRN's other development projects in the future" . Crisp and Martin further state that the QIPs package will provide PEN-PAR with "a laboratory to progressively assume the roles of UNHCR and IRC.... By the end of the QIPs, the Nicaraguan government will have its own operative regional and municipal mechanism for the management and follow up of its projects, particularly under the CIREFCA framework".

A review of QIPs suggests that there is no ground for such optimism. The authors of the review state that contrary to UNHCR's plans, it is doubtful whether the PARs will be able to play this role. The success and effectiveness of the PARs was a function of "the funding, training, guidance and supervision provided by UNHCR" (ibid). The PARs were formally incorporated into PRN in March 1992. However, it is pointed out that there has been "negligible contact between the two structures. PAR staff continue to relate more directly to UNHCR than to the PRN".

Notably, following UNHCR's withdrawal, many people involved in the QIPs predict that the "PARs will either collapse through a lack of resources, or that the existing, very competent PAR personnel will be replaced with political or personal appointees" The Nicaraguan government was positively predisposed to UNHCR, the number of returnees was relatively small (73,000), repatriation took place in the context of a restored peace, and the country offered "a relatively wide range of appropriate human, material, and organizational resources". These factors are lacking in most countries of return, and financial and managerial problems in the post-handover phase are likely to be worse in places like Afghanistan, Ethiopia, and Eritrea, to name but a few cases.

The third critical strategy identified by the Executive Committee of the High Commissioner's Programme to bridge the gap between humanitarian responses and development programmes is to include areas of return in national plans of development. The assumptions underlying this plea are, firstly, that there are national plans of development in all countries of return, and secondly, that there is the political will on the part of governments of the countries to which refugees return to include such areas in national development plans. In most countries of return, there may not be any meaningful ongoing national plans with which to link reintegration programmes, and the existence of political will also cannot be taken for granted. Even in countries such as Nicaragua, where there are well-developed human, organizational and material resources, the QIPs are not incorporated in national development, plans. In fact, according the UNHCR's Central Evaluation Section, the Nicaraguan government's role in the QIP initiative was minimal.

Crisp and Mayne note that "official structures have assisted to some extent in setting priorities for the programme as a whole, but they have not played a major role in the formulation, approval and execution of projects." In Cambodia, the linkage between UNHCR's reintegration programme and national rehabilitation and reconstruction efforts was even weaker, and this is likely to be the case in most countries whose economies have been devastated by war and civil strife.

The available evidence from Nicaragua demonstrates that following UNHCR's withdrawal, "beneficiaries may begin to divide up, consume, or sell the project resources which they control". In one development official's view, only five percent of the three hundred QIPs will be adopted and supported by development organizations. This is in spite of the fact that the prerequisite for constructing, reconstructing, and repairing of any facility was a formal commitment from the relevant line ministries or departments regarding staffing, maintenance, and recurrent costs. Compared to other countries of return in Africa and Southeast Asia, the Nicaraguan government is far better off and is able to maintain the facilities, yet "examples can be found of hospitals and health centres which are unable to secure an adequate supply of drugs and equipment".

To sum up, the refugee problem at global canvas is on rise despite growth and development of world economy under the current wave of privatisation, liberalisation and globalisation. Though cold war has virtually died, yet the dominating attitude of bigh powers (if not super) is disturbing the world peace and refugee population is also growthing. Instead of reaching statutory measures, the authoritarian behaviour of state must be checked.

Bibliography

Amnesty International (1997) *Refugees: Human Rights Have No Borders*. New York: Amnesty International Publications.

Bayefsky, Anne F. And Joan Fitzpatrick, eds. (2000) *Human Rights and Forced Displacement*. The Hague, Boston, and London: Martinus Nijhoff Publishers.

Bertrand, Maurice and Daniel Warner, eds. (1997) *A New Charter for a Worldwide Organization*? Dordrecht: Martinus Nijhoff.

Black, Richard (1998) *Refugees, Environment, and Development*. Essex, United Kingdom: Addison Wesley Longman Ltd.

Cernea, Michael Internal Refugee Flows and Development-Induced Population Displacement. *Journal of Refugee Studies* 3(4):320-339.

Cernea, Michael M. (1988) *Involuntary Resettlement in Development Projects: Policy Guidelines in World Bank-Financed Projects*. World Bank Technical Paper Number 80. Washington, D.C.: World Bank.

Cernea, Michael M. (1991) Involuntary Resettlement: Social Research, Policy, and Planning. In *Putting People First: Sociological Variables in Rural Development* (Second Edition). Michael M. Cernea, ed. pp. 188-215. New York: Oxford University Press.

Cernea, Michael M. (1995) Understanding and Preventing Impoverishment from Displacement: Reflections from the State of Knowledge. *Journal of Refugee Studies* 8(3):245-264.

Cernea, Michael M. (1997) The Risks and Reconstruction Model for Resettling Displaced Populations. World Development 25(10):1569-1587.

Cernea, Michael M., ed. (1999) *The Economics of Involuntary Resettlement: Questions and Challenges*. Washington, D.C.: The World Bank.

Cernea, Michael M. and Scott E. Guggenheim, eds. (1993) *Anthropological Approaches to Resettlement: Policy, Practice, and Theory*. Boulder, Colorado: Westview Press.

Chambers, Robert (1969) *Settlement Schemes in Tropical Africa.* New York, New York: Praeger.

Chambers, Robert, ed. (1970) *The Social Consequences of Resettlement*. London: Pall Mall Press.

Chambers, Robert (1986) Hidden Losers? The Impact of Rural Refugees and Refugee Programs on Poorer Hosts. *International Migration Review* 20:245-265.

Clark, Sam, Elizabeth Colson, James Lee, and Thayer Scudder (1995) Ten Thousand Tonga: A Longitudinal Anthropological Study from Southern Zambia, 1956-1991. *Population Studies* 49(1):91-109.

Cohen, Roberta and Francis M., eds. (1998) *The Forsaken People: Case Studies of the Internally Displaced*. Washington, D.C.: Brookings Institution Press.

Colson, Elizabeth (1971) *The Social Consequences of Resettlement: The Impact of the Kariba Resettlement Experience Upon the Gwembe Tonga*. New York and Oxford: Oxford University Press.

Cook, Cynthia, ed. (1994) *Involuntary Resettlement in Development Projects: Selected Papers fro, a Conference on Environment and Settlement Issues in Africa*. World Bank Technical Paper No. 237. Washington, D.C.: The World Bank.

Cuny, F., B. Stein, and P. Reed, eds. (1992) *Repatriation During Conflict in Africa and Asia*. Dallas: Center for the Study of Societies in Crisis.

De Waal, Alex (1997) *Famine Crimes: Politics and the Disaster Relief Industry in Africa*. London: James Currey and International African Institute.

Dorcey, Tony, with Achim Steiner, Michael Acreman, and Brett Orlando, eds. (1997) *Large Dams: Learning from the Past, Looking at the Future*. Gland, Switzerland: IUCN (the World Conservation Union) and Washington, D.C.: The World Bank.

Duffield, M. And J. Prendergast (1994) *Without Troops and Talks: Humanitarian Intervention in Ethiopia and Eritrea*. Lawrenceville, New Jersey: The Red Sea Press.

Erickson, Laurel (1998) An Assessment of Adjustment Strategies and Satisfaction with Cultural Orientation of Female Refugees: A Qualitative Comparison Between Refugees from Iraq and the Former Soviet Union in a Midwestern American City (Lincoln, Nebraska). M.A. Thesis, University of Nebraska-Lincoln, Lincoln, Nebraska.

Farer, Tom J. (1995) How the International System Copes with Involuntary Migration: Norms, Institutions, and State Practice. *Human Rights Quarterly* 17(1):72-100.

Ferris, E. (1993) *Beyond Borders: Refugees, Migrants, and Human Rights in the Post-Cold War Era*. Trenton, New Jersey: The Red Sea Press and Geneva: the WCC Press.

Giles, W. And H. Moussa, eds. (1996) *Development and Diaspora: Gender and the Refugee Experience*. Dudas, Ontario, Canada: Artemis Publishers.

Gold, Steven (1992) *Refugee Communities*. Newbury Park, California: Sage Publications.

Gordenker, Leon (1987) *Refugees in International Politics*. London and Sydney: Croom Helm.

Gersony, Robert (1989) *Why Somalis Flee: Synthesis of Accounts of Conflict Experience in Northern Somalia by Somali Refugees, Displaced Persons, and Others*. Report to the Bureau for Refugee Programs, Department of State, Washington, D.C.

Gowlland, Vera (1995) *The Problem of Refugees in the Light of Contemporary International Law Issues*. Dordrecht: Martinus Nijhoff.

Hansen, Art and Anthony Oliver-Smith, eds. (1982) *Involuntary Migration and Resettlement: The Problems and Responses of Dislocated People*. Boulder, Colorado: Westview Press.

Hampton, Janie (1998) *Internally Displaced People: A Global Survey*. London: Earthscan Publications.

Hitchcock, Robert K. (2001) *Anthropological Study on the Potential Impact of Refugees in M'Kata, Namibia*. Windhoek, Namibia: United Nations High Commissioner for Refugees.

Hitchcock, Robert K. and Hassan Hussein (1987) Agricultural and Non-Agricultural Settlements for Drought-Afflicted Pastoralists in Somalia. *Disasters* 11(1):30-39.

Holtzman, Jon D. (2000) *Nuer Journeys, Nuer Lives: Sudanese Refugees in Minnesota*. Boston: Allyn and Bacon.

Horowitz, Michael M. (1989) Victims of Development. *Development Anthropology Network* 7(2):1-8.

Horowitz, Michael M. (1991) Victims Upstream and Down. *Journal of Refugee Studies* 4(2):164-181.

Hyndman, Jennifer (2000) *Managing Displacement: Refugees and the Politics of Humanitarianism*. Minneapolis: University of Minnesota Press.

International Organization for Migration (1992) *Migration*

and the Environment. Background Paper. Washington, D.C.: The Refugee Policy Group.

International Organization for Migration (1996) *Environmentally-Induced Population Displacements and Environmental Impacts Resulting from Mass Migrations*. Geneva: United Nations High Commissioner for Refugees, the International Organization for Migration, and the Refugee Policy Group.

Jacobson, J. (1988) *Environmental Refugees: A Yardstick of Habitability*. Worldwatch Paper No. 86. Washington, D.C.: WorldWatch Institute.

Jean, Francois, ed. (1992) *Populations in Danger: Medecins San Frontieres*. London: John Libbey and Company.

Kane, Hal (1995) *The Hour of Departure; The Forces that Create Refugees and Migrants*. Worldwatch Paper 125. Washington, D.C.: Worldwatch Institute.

Kibreab, G. (1996) *Ready and Willing . . . But Still Waiting: Eritrean Refugees in Sudan and the Dilemma of Return*. Uppsala, Sweden: Life and Peace Research Institute.

Kibreab, G. (1997) Environmental Causes and Impact of Refugee Movements: A Critique of the Current Debate. *Disasters* 21(1):20-38.

Kleber, Rolf J., Charles R. Figley, and Berthold P.R. Gersons, eds. (1995) *Beyond Trauma: Cultural and Societal Dynamics*. New York and London: Plenum Press.

Koehn, Peter H. (1991) *Refugees from Revolution: U.S. Policy and Third-World Migration*. Boulder, Colorado: Westview Press.

Kourula, Pirkko (1997) *Broadening the Edges: Refugee Definition and International Protection Revisited*. The Hague: Martinus Nijhoff.

Lawson, Michael L. (1994) *Dammed Indians: The Pick Sloan Project and the Missouri River Sioux, 1944-1980*. Second Edition. Norman: University of Oklahoma Press.

Lesotho Highlands Development Authority (1997) Kingdom of Lesotho, Lesotho Highlands Water Project, Compensation Policy. Maseru, Lesotho: Lesotho Highlands Development Authority.

Loescher, Gil (1993) *Beyond Charity: International Cooperation and the Global Refugee Crisis*. Oxford: Oxford University Press.

Macklin, Audrey (1995) Refugee Women and the Imperative of Categories. *Human Rights Quarterly* 17(2):213-277.

Mayotte, J.A. (1992) *Disposable People? The Plight of Refugees*. Maryknoll, New York: Orbis Books.

McCully, Patrick (2001) *Silenced Rivers: The Ecology and Politics of Large Dams*. Second Edition. London and Atlantic Highlands, New Jersey: Zed Books.

McMillan, Della E. (1995) *Sahel Visions: Planned Settlement and River Blindness Control in Burkina Faso*. Tucson: University of Arizona Press.

McMillan, Della E., Thomas Painter, and Thayer Scudder (1992) *Settlement and Development in the River Blindness Control Zone*. World Bank Technical Paper No. 192. Washington, D.C.: World Bank.

McSpadden, Lucia Ann (2000) *Negotiating Return: Conflict and Control in the Repatriation of Eritrean Refugees*. Uppsala, Sweden: Life and Peace Research Institute.

Mollica, Richard F. (1988) The Trauma Story: The Psychiatric Care of Refugee Survivors of Violence and Torture. In *Post-Traumatic Therapy and Victims of Violence*, Frank M. Ochberg, ed. Pp. 295-314. New York: Brunner/Mazel.

Nicholson, Frances and Patrick Twomey, eds. (1999) *Refugee Rights and Realities: Evolving International Concepts and Regimes.* Cambridge: Cambridge University Press.

Pipher, Mary (2002) *The Middle of Everywhere: The World's Refugees Come to Our Town.* New York and London: Harcourt, Inc.

Rogers, R. And E. Copeland (1993) *Forced Migration: Policy Issues in the Post-Cold War World.* Medford, Massachusetts: The Fletcher School of Law and Diplomacy, Tufts University.

Scudder, Thayer (1962) *The Ecology of the Gwembe Tonga.* Manchester: Manchester University Press for the Rhodes-Livingstone Institute.

Scudder, Thayer (1973) The Human Ecology of Big Projects: River Basin Development and Resettlement. *Annual Review of Anthropology* 4:45-55.

Scudder, Thayer (1980) River-Basin Development and Local Initiative in African Savanna Environments. In *Human Ecology in Savanna Environments,* David Harris, ed. pp. 383-405. New York: Academic Press.

Scudder, Thayer (1981a) What It Means to Be Dammed: The Anthropology of Large-Scale Development Projects in the Tropics and Sub-Tropics. *Engineering and Science* 54(4):9-15.

Scudder, Thayer (1981b) *From Relief to Development: Some Comments on Refugee and Other Settlement in Somalia.* Report to the United States Agency for International Development, Mogadishu, Somalia.

Scudder, Thayer (1989) Conservation Vs. Development: River Basin Projects in Africa. *Environment* 31(2):4-9, 27-32.

Scudder Thayer (1990) Victims of Development Revisited:

The Political Costs of River Basin Development. *IDA Development Anthropology Network* 8(1):1-5.

Scudder, Thayer (1991a) The Need and Justification for Maintaining Trans-Boundary Flood Regimes: The Africa Case. Natural Resources Journal 31(1):75-107.

Scudder, Thayer (1997b) Resettlement. In *Water Resources: Environmental Planning, Management, and Development*, Asit K. Biswas, ed. Pp. 667-710. London: Macmillan.

Scudder, Thayer and Elizabeth Colson (1979) Long-term Research in the Gwembe Valley, Zambia. In *Long-term Field Research in Social Anthropology*, George Forster, Thayer Scudder, Elizabeth Colson, and Robert V. Kemper, eds. Pp. 227-254. New York, Academic Press.

Seymour, Frances J. And Vir Singh (1995) *A Preliminary Review of Experience with Resettlement to Achieve Conservation Objectives*. Washington, D.C.: World Wildlife Fund.

United Nations High Commissioner for Refugees (1998) *The State of the World's Refugees: A Humanitarian Agenda*. Oxford: Oxford University Press.

United States Committee for Refugees (1995) *World Refugee Survey*. Washington, D.C.: Immigration and Refugee Services of America.

United States Committee for Refugees (1997) *World Refugee Survey*. Washington, D.C.: Immigration and Refugee Services of America.

United Nations Development Program (2000) *Human Rights and Human Development: 2000 Human Development Program*. New York: United Nations.

Van der Veer, Guus (1998) *Counseling and Therapy with Refugees and Victims of Trauma: Psychological Problems of Victims of War, Torture, and Repression*. Second Edition. Chichester and New York: John Wiley and Sons.

Warner, Daniel, ed. (1995) *New Dimensions of Peacekeeping*. Dordrecht: Martinus Nijhoff.

Weiner, Myron (1995) *The Global Migration Crisis: Challenge to States and to Human Rights*. New York: Addison-Wesley Longman Publishers.

Wood, William B. (1994) Forced Migration: Local Conflicts and International Dilemmas. *Annals of the Association of American Geographers* 84(4):607-634.

World Bank (1990) Operational Directive 4.30: Involuntary Resettlement. *World Bank Operational Manual*. Washington, D.C.: World Bank.

World Bank (1993b) *Early Experience in Involuntary Resettlement: Overview*. Report No. 12142, June 1993. Washington, D.C.: World Bank.

Glossary

Asylum seeker: An asylum seeker is someone who has lodged an application for protection on the basis of the Refugee Convention or Article 3 of the ECHR.

Asylum Support Adjudicators: Asylum Support Adjudicators consider appeals by asylum seekers against UKBA decisions to refuse or terminate asylum support.

Certificate of Travel: Certificate of Travel, also known as the 'Home Office travel document' can be issued to people who have humanitarian protection or discretionary leave. The Certificate of Travel is not valid to travel to the country of origin.

Convention Travel Document (CTD): A Convention Travel Document, also known as 'blue document' is given to people with refugee status to use as a valid travel document in place of passport to travel overseas. This document is valid for all countries except the one from which the person sought asylum.

Dublin II Regulation: Dublin II Regulation provides EU member states with a mechanism for allocating responsibility to a single member state for processing an asylum claim.

European Convention on Human Rights (ECHR): The ECHR is an international legal instrument adopted under the auspices of the Council of Europe. Its provisions are enforceable in UK law courts.

Explore and Prepare: 'Explore and Prepare' is a Government funded programme which allows a group of refugees to visit their country of origin to assess the situation and prepare for their permanent return.

Family reunion: Family reunion is the policy enabling people bring their spouse and dependent children join them in the UK.

Human Rights Act 1998: The Human Rights Act incorporated the European Convention on Human Rights (ECHR) into the UK law.

Humanitarian protection (HP): Humanitarian protection is a form of immigration status. It is granted by the Home Office to a person who it decides has a need for protection but who does not meet the criteria for refugee status.

Immigration judge: An immigration judge is a person appointed by the Lord Chancellor to decide appeals made to the Asylum and Immigration Tribunal.

Immigration service: The Immigration Service is the UKBA department that regulates entry at UK ports, screens asylum seekers, manages asylum cases and contact with asylum seekers, and enforces removal of people who don't have.permission to remain in the country.

Indefinite leave to remain (ILR): ILR is a form of immigration status given by the UK Border Agency. Indefinite leave to remain (ILR) is also called 'permanent residence' or 'settled status' as it gives permission to stay in the UK on a permanent basis.

Integration loans: Integration loans are available to people who have been granted refugee status or humanitarian protection.

Legal representative: Legal representative is a barrister or a solicitor, solicitor's employee or other authorised person who acts for an applicant or appellant in relation to a claim.

NASS 35: A NASS 35 is a UKBA document which states that the holder is no longer entitled to support as they have received a positive decision on their asylum application. It is used to demonstrate that they are eligible for welfare benefits.

Naturalisation: Naturalisation is the process of becoming a British national.

New Asylum Model (NAM): The New Asylum Model was introduced by the UKBA for all new asylum claims in April 2007. NAM entails a 'case owner' from the UKBA who is responsible for processing the application from beginning to end.

Non-suspensive appeals (NSA): When a claim for asylum falls under the non-suspensive appeals process it means that the applicant only has the right to appeal against a negative UKBA decision once outside of the UK.

Office of the Immigration Services Commissioner: The Commissioner regulates immigration advice in the UK.

One stop appeal: The one stop appeal procedure aims to ensure that all grounds for appeal are dealt at one appeal only.

One Stop Service: One Stop Services are provided by the Asylum Support Partnership under contract with the UKBA. See 'Asylum Support Partnership'.

Port applicant: A person who applies for asylum to the immigration officer at an airport or seaport when she/he first arrives, ie. before passing through immigration control.

Refugee: A refugee is a person who 'owing to a well-founded fear of being persecuted for reasons of race, religion, nationality, membership of a particular social group, or political opinion, is outside the country of his nationality, and is unable to or, owing to such fear, is unwilling to avail himself of the protection of that country...' (Definition quoted from the 1951 Refugee Convention)

Refugee Convention: Refugee Convention means the United Nations Convention Relating to the Status of Refugees 1951 and the 1967 Protocol.

Refugee status: Refugee status is awarded to someone the UKBA recognises as a refugee as described in the Refugee Convention.

Statement of evidence form (SEF): A UKBA form which separated children applying for asylum use to set out their grounds for claiming asylum. The form was previously used for all asylum seekers.

Index